W9-BVQ-972

LIFE IN THE CITY OF DIRTY WATER

A MEMOIR OF HEALING

CLAYTON THOMAS-MÜLLER

ALLEN
LANE

ALLEN LANE

an imprint of Penguin Canada, a division of Penguin Random House Canada Limited

Canada • USA • UK • Ireland • Australia • New Zealand • India • South Africa • China

First published 2021

www.penguinrandomhouse.ca

LIBRARY AND ARCHIVES CANADA
CATALOGUING IN PUBLICATION

Title: Life in the city of dirty water : a memoir of healing /
Clayton Thomas-Muller.
Names: Thomas-Müller, Clayton, author.
Identifiers: Canadiana (print) 2020023675X |
Canadiana (ebook) 20200236903 | ISBN 9780735240063
(hardcover) | ISBN 9780735240070 (EPUB)
Subjects: LCSH: Thomas-Müller, Clayton. |
LCSH: Environmentalists—Canada—Biography.
| LCGFT: Autobiographies.
Classification: LCC GE56.T56 A3 2020 | DDC 333.72092—dc23

Book design by Kelly Hill
Cover design by Kelly Hill
Cover art: *Our Lives are in the Land* by Christi Belcourt
Interior artwork © Christi Belcourt except the image of
Inner Child on page 225 created by Isaac Murdoch

Printed in the United States of America

10 9 8 7 6 5 4 3 2

Penguin
Random
House

ALLEN
LANE

To Charlton Edward Budd,

You taught me how to hustle.
You taught me how to survive.
See you in the good hunting grounds.

CONTENTS

A NOTE FROM NI MAMA (MY MOTHER)

IN JANUARY 1977, I made one of the most difficult decisions of my life, which was to move to Winnipeg, Manitoba, in the pursuit of a better life for me and my unborn child. I left my family, friends, and everything that I was accustomed to. I was sixteen. Those first six months were difficult, to say the least. I found myself living in the confinement of an institution and all its rules. This was not foreign for me, as I had spent seven years in residential school, from the age of six to thirteen. What I found very difficult was the loneliness I once again felt deep within my soul, missing my family.

I wish I could tell you that life for me and my son Clayton magically changed once I moved to the city, but as for so many of our Indigenous brothers, sisters, and families who moved to the city in search of a better life, we faced many obstacles and tragedies.

This is not my story. *Life in the City of Dirty Water* is my son's story of growing up Indigenous in Winnipeg. Each one of us has a story to tell, and it is important that it be told through their own lens. I have fully supported my son throughout this transmedia project, felt his pain, laughed and cried as he wrote and produced this project. He has my full support and permission to share his story; as his mother, that is the gift I can give him at this junction in his life.

My son is an incredible speaker, but more importantly, a wonderful father, son, brother, uncle, and friend. He is resilient, intelligent, kind, courageous, and multi-talented. I couldn't imagine walking this journey of life without him. Thank you, Creator, for the gift you blessed me with forty-two years ago. Thank you, my son, for having the foresight and fortitude to share your journey with the intent of bringing awareness and healing.

Gail Pelletier
Winnipeg, Manitoba

tapasîwin

———

ᑕᐸᓯᐃᐧᐣ

———

flight

The first time my father saw an airplane, he thought it must be an angel. He was five years old, standing outside his family's cabin deep in the bush, on Pukatawagan First Nation in northern Manitoba. It was before he attended residential school, but Catholicism was already very present in the community and he had heard about angels from the priest who lived on the rez. That day, he heard a strange noise and looked up. He saw a white cross flying through the sky, and he thought: *This must be an angel, because what else could it be?*

He told me that story many years later. We were at the St. Regis Hotel in Winnipeg, and he was drunk out of his tree. It was one of the half-dozen times I ever spent with him. Even though I was only seven at the time, hearing the story triggered something inside me. I now know that the unsettled feeling I had was the sudden understanding that I'm only one generation away from living in the bush and being of the land. In only one lifetime, everything had changed.

My father, Peter Sinclair Sr., was a Cree bushman, and a miner, and he worked for the railroad. He was also an advisor to political leaders, and a writer, and a bureaucrat. He was from Pukatawagan First Nation, the easternmost First Nation in our territory, Treaty 6, which spans Saskatchewan and into Alberta. My family is spread out over a vast region, from Pelican Narrows to Sandy Bay, a Métis settlement in northern Saskatchewan, through South Indian Lake and Nelson House, Manitoba, where my mother's father comes from, with Pukatawagan right in the middle of it all. These are all the territories of the Swampy Cree people, or the Rocky Cree as we call ourselves.

My father was actually half Cree. His father, Keno, born Adalbert du Bois de Vroylande, was a full-blooded Belgian immigrant who was a World War II fighter pilot and a war hero. My grandfather became disillusioned with his aristocratic life and jumped on a steamship after the war. He went to Hudson Bay, got on a dogsled, and went into the bush. He met a woman who became his wife, and they created my father. My grandfather was famous in our community of Pukatawagan. He and my grandmother owned and operated a general store. He had a Clydesdale horse way up in northern Manitoba, and he built a root cellar so he could have vegetables in the wintertime. That just blew all the Indians away.

My father drank himself to death at the age of fifty-eight. I don't know why he drank, but the limited stories he told me about himself give a glimpse: watching his father die of a heart attack in their general store, being raped by a nun throughout his whole time in residential school.

The last time I saw my father was at the Seven Oaks General Hospital in Winnipeg. He still had jet-black hair and big, bushy black eyebrows, sort of a kind look, and a bit of a crooked smile. But he was all swollen and yellow with jaundice. The late stages of cirrhosis had kicked in. The last thing he said to me was "Ah, Clayton, always so serious. I'm sorry I haven't been a good dad. Take care of your kids. Make some money so that when you're dead, they'll have something."

I said, "OK, I'll do that, Dad," and I left. I was twenty-six years old.

A couple of weeks later, I flew back to Winnipeg to bury him. As I sat on the plane, I thought back to my father's memory of the first plane he saw and here I was sitting in one of those white crosses in the sky on my way to bury him.

After the funeral, I drove with the procession to The Pas for the second funeral, with my dad's body in a coffin in the back of a pickup leading the way. I slept beside his body at the funeral parlour in Opaskwayak Cree Nation, and then my siblings brought him to our trapline for his third and final funeral service, burying him beside our grandmother. His spirit sat with me for the drive back to Winnipeg, the whole way down Highway 6, and we laughed about all the things we did not get to work out while he was still alive.

I didn't really know my dad, but I was always thankful to him for giving me life. I never hated him for being a drunk and for not achieving his potential. He had been a very handsome man, intelligent and articulate. People I've talked to from his generation have told me that they thought he was going to be the one to lead our people.

From my father, I have eleven brothers and six sisters, from Alaska to New York and all the way to Brazil. I know a few of them and we all have different moms. All of my dad's children took his death differently—some got angry, some didn't come to the funerals, some were so drunk they were barely there. Some fought over my dad's earthly possessions, and he didn't have much. The only thing I inherited from my father was the sports coat he had on when he was admitted into the hospital before he died. It still had his blood all over the front of it from him puking it up. What I really wanted was photos—I only have one or two of my dad, and he was pretty hammered in them. I don't have any pictures of him looking dignified.

My dad had an eye for my mom, though he was much older than her. He first met her in 1976, when my mom was about fifteen and going to high school in Thompson, way up in northern Manitoba. At the time, my father was working as an agent for the federal Ministry of Indian Affairs. He was one of the only Indian Indian agents.

On one of his trips to Thompson, he ran into my mom and he said to her, "Hey Gail, I really like you. I would like to spend some time with you." That night he took her on a date to the Thompson Inn, a notorious Indian bar. He and my mom snagged on their first date. My mom became pregnant with me. She didn't tell him.

The social worker at Student Services at the Indian Affairs office in Thompson told my mom that she had to get an abortion. But my mom, like all my aunties, had gone to a Catholic residential school, so she thought she'd go to hell if she had an abortion. The social worker said, "Well, you're going to have a really hard time if you stay here in the north and have a baby." She put my mom on an airplane to Winnipeg.

My mom was all alone, with no friends or family, and over eight hundred kilometres from home. The social workers in Winnipeg managed to get her a place at Villa Rosa, a home for unwed mothers, run by nuns. She stayed there until the morning of July 17, 1977, when she thought she had to go to the washroom and one of her girlfriends said, "Maybe you should go to the hospital." The hospital was one block over, so she walked there. I was born at 8:42 that morning in a hospital called Misericordia, in the West Broadway neighbourhood of Winnipeg.

My mother is also Cree. Her mom came from Pukatawagan, and her dad is from Southend, Saskatchewan. My mother was born in The Pas, in northern Manitoba. She lived a trapping lifestyle in the bush until the RCMP took her from her family and forced her to attend the Guy Hill Indian Residential School. She was only six.

She stayed there until grade 10. My mother moved to Thompson to finish her high school at the Indian day school they had there. It was at that day school that she met my dad. So she pretty much went from residential school to the maternity ward.

But my mother left our reserve at sixteen. She knew that Winnipeg could offer her more than just decent healthcare. She wanted to get an education. She wanted to give her child more choices than she had. If she was going to raise a kid alone, Winnipeg was the place to do it. There were more services available and more education and work options in Winnipeg than back home on the rez. And people weren't trying to rape you or shoot you, which was a common thing in Puk back in the 1970s, which is why they called it Dodge City. It had the highest murder rate per capita in North America for a decade. She was vulnerable there. To my mom, going to the city was the safest thing for a pregnant teenager to do.

She lived a paradox I have spent years trying to understand. She had to leave her people to be safe. Leaving the land is the source of so many of our problems, so how could it also be the solution? She survived residential school only to seek refuge at a hospital founded by nuns. These facts have not been easy for me to reconcile.

Still, my mother did not turn her back on the land. My childhood was like that of many other Indigenous youth in this country called Canada—it was very urban. But when I was a young child, I would spend my summers in the north on our family's trapline in Jetait, which is at Mile 121 of the train line between Pukatawagan Cree Nation and Lynn Lake. A trapline is the land Indians are entitled to occupy under the Indian Act. Each trapper is allowed to hunt, fish, and trap on a parcel of land, and the head of the family receives a land occupancy permit, which is passed down through inheritance. So a trapline is a complicated thing too. It is part of an Indian's relationship with the federal government. But it is also a crucial part of their relationship with their family. And it is a life-giving relationship with the land.

Often, Mooshum Edward would take all the kids to walk his trapline. We would accompany him as he checked his rabbit snares. Ours is a land of wetlands and swamps that open up onto beautiful rivers and the rocky shorelines of lakes. It is a world of secrets, and of shadows pierced by shafts of sunlight and blue sky, of the earthy smell of sphagnum and the lemony aroma of spruce. We loved making our way along the paths and among the thickets.

Grandpa's snares would frequently catch animals he hadn't intended—a lot of squirrels and chipmunks, that sort of thing. We kids loved it. We'd get these stiff squirrels on a piece of copper wire and we'd walk behind my grandpa making the squirrels talk: "Hi, Larry, how you doing?" "Oh not too bad, Bob." "Going to the store today?" We'd make the squirrels fight. Make them fly. Kids are like that.

On our trapline, I got to witness the abundance of our land and the incredible love that my great-grandmother and great-grandfather had, not just for me but for so many children whom they would take from the reserve every summer to come live out in the bush and fish and pick berries. A lot of kids who had problems or came from dysfunctional homes would stay with my great-grandparents, who would take care of them, and feed them, and give them the love they needed.

My mother's grandfather used to have an old cabin down by the lake. It was a scary place, because if my great-grandpa started drinking, he would sit in that cabin. The kids weren't supposed to go down there when he was drinking. Sometimes, when he wasn't there, I'd go to that cabin with my cousins Starr and Rina, my auntie Isabel's daughters. Auntie Isabel was the daughter of my grandmother's sister, but she was basically a big sister to my mother. She took my mom in many times over the years and we would stay with them. Isabel married a Ukrainian man named Peter Pomart Zibida. They had five kids: Starr, Rina, and Peter Jr. plus two sons, Charlton and Ed, from Isabel's previous marriage. All my greatest memories—my most cherished memories—of my childhood are of being deep in the bush or on my great-grandparents' trapline in Jetait with Starr and Rina. They were more like sisters to me than cousins.

One time, when we were all young, Starr was picking raspberries and Rina and I were sitting on the roof of the cabin, stuffing our faces with berries. Suddenly, I started choking. I couldn't breathe. Rina thought I was faking and was patting me gently on the back, saying, "There, there, Clayton, don't choke." When Starr climbed up onto the roof and saw my face turning blue, she realized how serious it was. She slapped me really hard on the back and all this raspberry jam flew out of my mouth and I was able to breathe again.

Starr was the shining light of that family. She was my best friend growing up. She was one of the kindest and most empathetic human beings I've ever known, and tough too. She would never let me forget that she was a year older than me. When we were children, we had a childhood crush thing that we were going to get married. Of course, we knew that you don't marry your cousin, but that didn't matter to us when we were kids.

After I recovered from this scary feeling of almost dying, we cousins climbed down from the top of the cabin and walked through the meadow to go see what my great-grandmother was doing by the camp cooking fire outside their cabin. Surrounding us was a deep, impenetrable forest of whispering poplars, statuesque pines. Across a meadow filled with flowers, raspberry and blueberry bushes, and rose hips was the pathway to Jetait Lake. Behind my grandmother's cabin, the place we would go to shoot spruce chickens, the forest floor was covered with a deep, soft moss that our ancestors used to use to make diapers for babies. In one square metre of this muskeg, this soft metres-deep living organism that spans the entire boreal forest from northern British Columbia to eastern Quebec, are some of the highest concentrations of medicinal plants and cranberries and blueberries, and burrows for dozens and dozens of animals. Our trapline was truly a beautiful place for children to play and learn about biology, or what we call the circle of life.

I drowned when I was a little boy. We were out on Midnight Lake near our trapline in Jetait, a hundred miles from civilization. My uncle Alec had been drinking and we were horsing around. Alec was a bit of a trickster. We were out in the canoe, splashing each other with paddles, and my auntie Bernadette was laughing and my mom was saying, "Stop fucking around!" It was broad daylight and a big snowy owl flew real low over the canoe. We all stopped, suddenly really scared, because we knew the omens around owls being messengers of death.

Then Uncle Alec pulled out his shotgun and took a shot. Auntie Bernadette yelled, "What the fuck are you doing? You don't shoot no owl!" He was laughing. All of a sudden, water was rushing into the canoe. My next memory is coughing and coughing and opening my eyes and there, leaning over with his little hands on his knees, looking at me right in my eyes, was my brother Perry, who grew up to be our Sundance chief at our family's Sundance in Mokoman River. He'd heard a commotion out on the water and he came running down to the shoreline and my mom was there, resuscitating me. Bringing me back to life.

My great-grandmother died suspiciously on our reservation when I was a little boy. Some say she died from accidental choking, however there are other rumours that she was murdered. My great-grandfather died shortly after she died, as is the case with so many lifelong couples. My great-grandparents were the core of our family, and when they were gone, my mother and her siblings all fell apart a little bit. They got into drinking and became less grounded.

We were all less grounded. After my great-grandparents passed away, my mother stopped taking me up north. That led to a very challenging time for all of us. The further away from my great-grandparents that my mother and her siblings got, the more vulnerable they became to pressures that come from living in the city—going out and partying, hanging out with people who were bad influences. My mom was just a kid.

The more time passed, the more that grounding connection of the north melted away. Summer is the time of plenty, to go up north, to connect with our living ancestors, to connect with the land, to eat and drink from the land. But we were more and more cut off from that.

The way I picture it is that the synapses of our brains run on electric energy, and when you're in the city, you have the thick layer of concrete dividing your body from the sacredness of the Earth. Your energy and mental processes become muddled and confused. When we stopped going up north, a string of dark years began for me and my mother.

My mom was involved in some abusive relationships when I was a child and it was an incredibly difficult time for both of us. Many of the men were physically violent to my mother. They would go at it and my mom would always end up being the one who got really hurt. She was put in the hospital many, many times. She was almost killed many times. I would watch all of this. I got really used to it. Usually the most violent of her partners would just leave after moments of extreme violence, but once my mom healed, they would always track us down and the cycle would start all over again.

My mom tried to keep me connected to our culture, but it was sporadic. She took me to get my spirit name as a baby. She took me to pow wows, protests, and events in the Native community. But what young boy or young man truly understands ceremony, or the wisdom of Elders? But without that connection to the land, much of my experiences with our shared Native culture felt hollow or ornamental. My culture was slipping through my fingers.

Our world seems to take a special delight in destroying culture, but few of us know what life is like without tradition to make sense of it. The few glimpses of my own people's ceremony felt hollow and weird, even shameful and dirty. How could that be? I wasn't used to seeing Native people being Native people. I hadn't seen that since I was up north with my grandparents. And it was different there, because they were Catholic but they were the most Native Native people I had ever met. It was a bizarre thing to see real live Native people dancing pow wow, or doing ceremony, or especially asserting their rights in protest because every little Native kid deals with being told that their people have disappeared, they no longer exist, they are just a page in a social studies history book.

What I knew of Native people at that time, when I was a little boy, was that we liked eating pemmican, we were transient, and we were unsophisticated and somehow dirty. People still call us savage, but they used that word a lot more then. Going once in a while to a Native event in the city, with all of that on my shoulders and deep inside my psyche, is no substitute for a relationship with the land. So it felt hollow.

The funny thing is, many of us living in the city were careful to protect our sense of identity by performing our ceremonies, while our relatives back up north may have given them up. There were city Natives who knew how to pray in a sweat lodge but would succumb to exposure overnight in the bush, and there were their cousins who speak Cree and live off the land but have little Western education and may not know or perform the ceremonies. Which one is more Native? When I was a child, it was one or the other.

Because my mom was completing her education and working, I was a latchkey kid. I would come home from school with my key around my neck and there would be a twenty-dollar bill with a note: "Order some pizza. I'll see you at 9. Love you, Mom." After my mom came home, she would be up until the late hours doing papers for her university courses and her college diploma in psychiatric nursing.

My mother was very abusive when I was a little boy. After a couple of violent incidents with me, she got help and was given prescription drugs to help stabilize her. Violence was something she knew well. She had learned it in residential school. She had learned it at home. Now she was teaching me.

I remember trying to talk to her late one night and she didn't make any sense. She said something about Tarzan not getting his way and went back to sleep. When she was going to nursing school, I dreaded the weekends because they were preceded by promises to do fun things, but once she and my aunties started partying, I wouldn't see her until the wee hours of the morning, and usually she was with a date and my Saturday plans with her would be scratched. It was the loneliest time of my life.

When I was really young, my mom was attending Daniel McIntyre high school, working towards completing grade 12 so she could go on to university. The summer she was eighteen, she worked as a drop-in youth worker with the Native Clan Organization in Winnipeg. The Native Clan Organization worked with ex-convicts at the old post office building and later established halfway houses.

My mom also worked at the Winnipeg Indian Council, on Burrows Avenue, in 1981. One of the people she worked with, David Chartrand, would become the president of the Manitoba Métis Federation. The Winnipeg Indian Council expanded and relocated to the former CPR station at Main and Higgins, changing its name to the Aboriginal Council of Winnipeg. It was one of a few inner-city advocacy organizations involved in delivering social programs for the urban Indigenous community.

One of the key people in this organization used to run a couple of group homes funded by what was then called the Children's Aid Society. Working in one of those group homes was a tall, charismatic guy named Roddy. He was handsome, and very proud of his Mohawk heritage. Soon he and my mom were together. He became the only dad I'd ever had.

He did try hard sometimes to do that right. I have many good memories of the things fathers and sons do. Camping in Birds Hill Park or at Grand Beach on Lake Winnipeg. Fishing on the Assiniboine River. I remember doing "laser fights" as Roddy and I stood side by side at the toilet. I remember him throwing me so high into the air I thought I could fly.

I never believed I'd grow up to be as strong or as manly as Roddy. He was phenomenally muscular. He had the biggest penis I've ever seen. It was ridiculous. It must have been at least ten inches long. I remember looking down at my chubby tummy and then looking at his pack and then looking at my tiny little penis and looking at his freaking massive penis and thinking: *Wow, why don't I look like my dad?* Of course, I was just a kid and he wasn't my biological father.

One time my dad went running and I ran with him to the end of the street. I said, "I want to come jogging with you. I want to learn how to do what you're doing." He said, "Naw. You can't keep up." I remember watching him continue to run when I stopped at the end of the street and being so angry watching him run down the road without me.

He was training for a fight. He was a champion boxer and kickboxer. He was a killing machine. He used to be light heavyweight champion Donny Lalonde's sparring partner, and I heard years later that he used to kick the shit out of Lalonde in the ring. I also hear from an old-timer of the Savoy Hotel—sometimes called the Indian Embassy, since there is a high concentration of Natives at the bar—that Roddy used to go in there to pick fights, and just destroy guys. None of that surprises me at all.

Unfortunately, his family was very dysfunctional and had within it much domestic violence. That explained why Roddy often reacted to normal situations with violence.

I remember once I was driving with Roddy. The car in front of us slowed down and then stopped. Roddy had to stomp on the brake, and that set him off. He got out of the car and approached the other driver, who had seen Roddy coming. Not that it did him any good. Roddy kicked him in the face, and the guy crumpled to the pavement, unconscious. I had seen him kick my mother just as hard. She had ended up in intensive care.

Roddy got back in the car and drove off. "Fucking guy didn't signal." That was Roddy.

My mom and Roddy had an apartment down Main Street, in an old building by the Ukrainian Orthodox church with its big black domes on top that look like onions. The apartment had many old windows and secret compartments behind the living room wall. On the bookshelf we had every single Hardy Boys hardcover.

I used to take off on my mom. I'd run downstairs in my diaper. There was a Dairi-Wip right outside in the parking lot and I'd go in there and the old Greek man running the shop would sit me up on the deep-freezer and give me an ice cream cone and call my mom and say, "Hey, your kid's here. He's eating ice cream. Come and get him." My mom would be like: *Oh my fucking god.* And she'd come get me.

Birds would land on the apple tree outside the living room window of the house on Arnold Street, where I lived when I was four. One day, I was watching cartoons, looking at the apple tree, looking at the birds, looking at the cartoons. The front door suddenly flew open and Roddy stormed in, really irate. My mom had been sleeping in her room, right in front of me. He yelled, "Gail, you open the door!" She screamed back, "I've got nothing to say to you!"

He started pounding on the locked door. Finally it shattered. Splintered wood was everywhere. I picked up two pieces of wood and I was pretending they were an airplane. I walked into the bedroom, where Roddy was beating my mom on the bed. She was screaming and there was blood everywhere. I went up to him and tugged on his shirt a little and he stopped and looked at me like: *What the fuck do you want?* I said, "Do you have any glue?" He yelled, "What?!" I said again, "Do you have any glue?" He screamed, "What do you need glue for?" I told him, "I want to glue this wing on this airplane so that I can fly away from here." He stopped and kind of snapped out of it. And he got up and walked out.

My uncle Peter, who was a Ukrainian guy and a real gentleman, would take me and my cousin Juno, also known as PJ or Peter Jr., to the Assiniboia Downs racetrack. He would say, "Hey, do you guys want to come with me to do something?" At that time, Juno was four or five, barely older than a toddler. I was eight years old. We would jump on the 24 Ness bus from downtown Winnipeg and ride for an hour and a half into the sticks. The old diesel buses back then were way nicer than the ones now. They were rounder and looked more art deco-y, bright orange with chrome.

The 24 bus would stop where the houses ended and farm fields began. We would walk across a field, with grain up to my chest, to get to the horse track. Uncle Peter would say, "You guys be cool, OK? Let's not tell Auntie what we did today. And if you keep your lips sealed, I'll get you a bowtie." A bowtie was the world's fanciest doughnut. It was a figure-eight doughnut, topped with chocolate with whipped cream on top and a maraschino cherry. They were a big deal. They were a dollar ten versus the normal fifty-cent doughnut. It was double the doughnut.

At the track they had this machine that had peanuts in the shell underneath a hot lamp. Those were the best peanuts I ever had in my life because they were warm. We'd eat peanuts and watch the horses. We'd go down to the stables to pick the horses to bet on. My uncle never won. We always got on the bus broke, but he always had money to buy us bowties. We'd go to the doughnut shop right by Central Park on Salter, and there'd be three or four bowties and no more. We'd say, "We want two bowties." We'd have to eat up the bowties before we got to the apartment so that the other cousins wouldn't see. Buying bowties for all of us would've cost ten dollars.

I always remember how happy my uncle Peter looked at the racetrack, being in his own space, having some privacy. They had five kids in a two-bedroom apartment. I regret that he passed away before I could express to him how special my memories are of him, going to watch the horse races at Assiniboia Downs.

Roddy worked at a group home on Barber Street. My dad had a sexual relationship with one of the girls in the group home, and while he was with her, he would leave me alone with one of the boys, Victor, who was a well-known sexual offender. He must have been around fourteen or fifteen years old. I was three or four.

The brain is a pretty amazing thing, the way it works to protect you from trauma. You black out memories that are violent. Most of my memories of Victor present him as very loving and caring. But I remember one night Roddy was working the night shift and he put me to sleep in Victor's room. I remember Victor sleeping behind me and pulling my pyjamas down and whispering into my ear while he raped me.

Victor also assaulted me at the Farm, another group home where my dad worked. Victor took me out to see the rabbits, who had just had babies. I remember looking into the cage and seeing that some of the babies had been bitten and killed, which I guess is what mama rabbits do if there are too many babies to nurse. Victor grabbed the dead bunnies and threw them out into the tall grass and whistled. The giant boars that lived on the farm came running and they ate those babies.

He took me to a shed where there were garden tools hanging on the wall. He laid me down on my stomach and pulled my pants down. I remember telling him that his pee-pee wouldn't fit in my bum. The next memory I have is running towards the farm with my pants around my ankles. I ran into a goat that had red eyes, and the goat chased me. I jumped on top of a haystack and I sat up there and I cried.

I told my mom what had happened, and she lost it on Roddy. They never pressed charges. No police were called.

When I was really young, my hero was the Incredible Hulk. I thought the Hulk was the most powerful thing ever, and I would pretend to be him all the time. My mother cut the feet off my onesies and shredded the ends so I looked like the Incredible Hulk. When my mom and my dad Roddy would have house parties and our house would fill up with big Indian guys with

1970s afros drinking Canadian Club whiskey, I would come out of my bedroom in my shredded onesie into a cloud of cigarette and weed smoke. I'd launch my toy car across the living room. People thought it was the cutest thing ever.

Winnipeg was designed as a grid city, so it's all tic-tac-toe in terms of how you navigate the streets. When you're a kid, wandering up the back alleys of Winnipeg is awesome. The streets downtown behind Portage Avenue all have back alleys and you can go and explore, dig in the dumpster, and find the strangest shit to play with.

Growing up, we spent a lot of the summer trying to escape the heat. Nobody I knew had air conditioning. I remember it being forty freaking degrees Celsius and super fucking humid and just wanting two things: a swimming pool and Dickie Dee ice cream. These ice cream boys would bike around with freezers on the front of their bikes. At that time fifty cents would get you an ice cream bar. Those tasted real good when it was plus forty. A lot of our time was spent trying to hustle up money to get a Dickie Dee, and maybe a Slurpee. Winnipeg is the Slurpee capital of the planet. Indians drink a helluva lot of Slurpees. Even in the dead of winter, minus forty, you'll see Natives walking into 7-Eleven in Central and walking out with these big fucking Slurpees. It's no wonder we got a problem with diabetes in our community. Slurpees are nothing but corn syrup, food colouring, and ice.

When we weren't hustling up money for a Dickie Dee, a lot of our time was spent trying to break into the swimming pool at the fancy apartment next door. They had an outdoor pool and quite often we would scale the wall. To scale the wall—which must have been close to twelve feet high—we would stand up on someone's back or get thrown up, or stand on someone's hand and then get up. You could kind of shimmy up and then throw your leg over. If we couldn't do that, we'd wait until somebody was coming out of the apartment and then we'd rush the door. Then we'd have to wait again in a hallway for someone to come out of the pool and then rush that door. There was no lifeguard there, just the other people who lived in the apartment, and nobody would ever rat out a bunch of little Indian kids for getting into a pool on a plus-forty day. But once in a while we would get caught trying to break into the apartment pool and we would be sent off.

Our backup was a fountain at Central Park, which is still there. It's a real beautiful old-school fountain, a real British colonial kind of fountain, like something out of Harry Potter. We would swim in that. Or we would take the long walk up Salter, which turns into Memorial Drive, to the legislature fountains. The legislature fountains is where the entire city of Winnipeg goes when it's a really hot day. In the later years the city installed razor floors so that you would really cut yourself if you jumped into the fountain. They've since removed them because a lot of people were upset about that, in the way that people got upset when cities put spikes under bridges so homeless people can't sleep there. They said, "Let the poor little Indian kids swim in the fountain. It's plus fucking forty."

When I was a kid, there was a popular program called *The Friendly Giant*. The Friendly Giant had this creepy chicken puppet that was in a bag and it would talk to him and his friend the giraffe, another creepy puppet that would stick his head through the window of the castle that he lived in. At the Friendly Giant's feet were miniature chairs and tables and a mini fireplace. I started having a fucked-up dream that still recurs. That Friendly Giant was chasing me with a knife. I knew if he caught me, he would molest me.

My mom tells a story of how I would say things in public and embarrass the shit out of her and my aunties. One time, I was in the choir in church, up in the front, and I yelled out, "My grandma drinks beer!" Another time I told everyone on the bus, "We've had stew all week!" My auntie Karen was trying to tell them, "No, we haven't," while I was yelling, "Yes, we did! Yes, we did!"

Next to my mother, my auntie Karen was the person I most cherished as a child. She was my mom's best friend. She lived with my mom and me at our apartment on Main Street when I was three. She moved in with us because she was having a baby. The only real memory I have of my auntie Karen, other than the feeling of her love, was that she'd come into my bed and she'd say, "Push over." I'd push over and I remember smelling her hair, which smelled like Head & Shoulders, and I remember feeling so safe.

My auntie Karen died during her pregnancy. She had an aneurysm and she and her baby passed away in her sleep. Her boyfriend never recovered from that.

Karen was my mom's baby sister. They both survived Indian residential school. They foraged at the Lynn Lake dump for something to eat when they were little kids. Her death kind of blew my mom's brain away. She was institutionalized for a while after Karen's death.

There was no one to take care of me then, so Roddy took me to Montreal because he was under investigation by Child and Family Services in Winnipeg due to that inappropriate sexual relationship with a young woman at one of the group homes where he was working. When we got to Montreal, he dropped me off at his mom's and then disappeared. Everybody called Roddy's mom Mom. Mom was a staunch Mohawk woman who told everybody she was Carib because Roddy's dad was a Carib man, though they were divorced. Mom was a colourful character who would send me parcels at Christmas addressed to "Master Clayton Thomas."

The whole time I was in Montreal, I kept thinking: *What is going on?* I didn't understand what anybody was saying. The neighbourhood kids spoke a different language. The only cartoons that were in English were *Hercules* and *Rocket Robin Hood*, which both kind of sucked. I remember riding the subway and being blown away by how futuristic it was. I remember cherry cola, and going to Schwartz's Deli, and poking the eyeballs of the fish that were packed in ice at the Atwater Market, thinking it was trippy: fish out of water. I also played with Raggedy Ann and Andy dolls to keep myself sane.

I didn't know where Roddy was for the months that I was in Montreal. My dad's sister sexually abused me when she would babysit me. When I told my dad's mom what had happened, she didn't call my dad and she didn't call the cops. But she did beat her daughter within an inch of her life with a baseball bat in front of me. There was blood all over the cream-coloured plush carpet. I was terrified. I thought Mom had killed my dad's sister. My dad's brother walked in when the beating was going down and I remember looking at him and thinking: *Help me*. But he just left. I don't think he could deal with how heavy the situation was. I didn't ever hold it against him because he was just a kid too. My dad's sister was in bed for days; she couldn't move. They didn't take her to the hospital. Mom told me to never talk about it.

Roddy returned to Montreal one day, out of nowhere. It turned out he had taken my mom's sister Rhona to Quebec City and he was messing around with her while my mom was in the mental hospital. Soon after my dad returned, I got into a fight with a kid down the street because the kid had taken my tricycle. I said, "Hey Dad, this guy took my bike. I told him to give it back but he doesn't speak English. He just speaks French so he doesn't know what I'm saying. Can you go get my bike?"

My dad said, "Fuck that. You go over there and you kick his ass right now."

I said, "What?"

He said, "You better go over there and kick his ass or I'll kick *your* ass."

So, in my OshKosh B'gosh corduroy overalls, I walked up the street and rolled up on this little francophone boy and popped him in the mouth and pushed him off my tricycle and rode back. Then my dad took me out for ice cream.

When I was five, my mom and I fled from Winnipeg to Brandon, Manitoba, in an attempt to escape from Roddy.

Brandon is where I spent a big part of my childhood, from kindergarten up to grade 5.

When we first got there, my mom and I lived with some of my aunties, and we spent a winter living in different rooming houses. We eventually moved into our first real home, a duplex at 20 Evergreen Boulevard, on the south side of Brandon. I have a lot of childhood memories from 20 Evergreen. Behind the houses there's a slough along the train tracks. The kids from the neighbourhood would play in the slough as the train was going by—it was a pretty healthy slough from an ecosystem perspective. We'd hunt for treasure in the little pools—mostly leeches and that kind of thing.

While my mom and I were living on Evergreen Boulevard, Roddy moved to Brandon to stalk my mom. I remember the smell of fear that came off my mom when we saw him in the supermarket.

Roddy and my mom tried to make it work again. He promised not to be violent with her and he broke that promise.

One of my most vivid memories of my childhood is when my mom abandoned me to go to a Mormon temple in Alberta with my auntie Isabel. Mom left me with a Native lady that she was friends with. The lady was nice, but I remember how much it bothered me. All Isabel's kids got to go to Alberta—my cousins Starr and Rina, my cousin Pete and everybody—but Isabel told my mom she couldn't bring me. My mom has always said she felt bad for leaving me behind. While she was gone, I was playing in a park, running around. I tripped and my knee went into a hole and got all cut up. When I pulled my knee out of the hole, I saw that there was some dead thing in the hole that was festering. The hole was filled with maggots, and the maggots were stuck to the blood on my knee. I remember looking at the maggots in the hole, looking at the scrape on my knee, looking at the maggots on my blood, and thinking: *Where the heck is my mom?*

On the streets where I grew up, it was telling how abuse would come up in the real world. I used to war with the little Native kids who lived at our end of Evergreen Boulevard. One day we'd be friends, and the next day we'd be fist-fighting. One time all us kids were playing on the crescent and an older brother was picking on me. Out of the corner of my eye, I saw my mom coming around the corner and I got brave. I started swinging for the fences and he bopped me right on the mouth and that was the end of that. Real quick, I went running back to see my mom. I was crying and she held me. She said, "My boy, you shouldn't be violent. Don't ever be like that. You should never be violent in that way." She said it in a really loving way. She held me close. She was guiding me through her words.

We lived in a duplex at the end of the crescent; there were a couple of other Native families living there as well. The duplexes where low income housing; there were three of them. The white folks who lived on Evergreen Boulevard all lived in single-dwelling houses farther up the street. My best buddy when I was five, a blond-haired, blue-eyed boy named Joel, lived in a blue house, number 6, up the street from us. Joel's mom was a really proper lady and she didn't like me because I had long hair and braids and I was about as brown as you could get. I used to fantasize about how cool things would be if I looked like Joel. Even at the age of five, I understood that having fair skin, blond hair, and blue eyes would mean life would be easier.

One time I was at Joel's, playing in the yard, and I knocked on the door and asked if I could use the washroom. Joel's mother said no, and Joel and I ran to my house down the street. I didn't make it to my house. I pooped and peed myself in front of Joel. Joel reassured me it was OK. He was a really nice kid. But after that day, whenever I'd knock on Joel's door, his mom would say that he wasn't around.

That was often my experience, whether it was at Linden Lanes School or Meadows School or Flemming elementary school, which is now a First Nations school known as Sioux Valley High School. My friendships with a lot of kids stopped after my friends' parents saw me.

Brandon is the home of the Wheat Kings, a Western Hockey League team. It's a farming town. There are way more people of colour living in Brandon now, but when I lived there, it was very much a white town. But not all white. The Dakota tribal council communities came to Brandon for business: Sioux Valley, Sioux reserves. I remember my mom and my aunties hating on all of them because my mom and my aunties were Cree. I shake my head now, but at the time I thought it was normal that the Sioux and the Cree should hate each other.

I'll never forget going to a party of one of my mom's Lakota girlfriends. I was friends with her son. When the party was over and everybody left, his mother, after drinking too much, became enraged with jealousy towards my mom. I watched her beat my mother bloody in their dining room and break her new expensive glasses. The whole event sucked because I was really good friends with that boy and he never talked to me again after that fight that our mothers had. I never did figure out why that woman beat my mother that night but my mother never talked to her again either.

There used to be an old Eastern European lady who lived in a house in Brandon and who everybody called Grandma. Any kid from the neighbourhood could go knock on her door and she would invite you into her house and there were toys and board games you could play with. She was forever baking raisin oatmeal cookies that she would give us kids to eat. She didn't say much. I don't think her family ever visited her so she opened her door to all the little Native kids in the neighbourhood, and was Grandma to all of us.

One time when I was eight years old, I knocked on her door and a bald guy, who I'd never seen in all the times I'd gone to Grandma's house, answered. I said, "Is Grandma here?" He said, "No. She's dead," and he slammed the door in my face. I was all by myself and I was devastated. For months after, I would walk by her house on my way to school. It was the first time that I experienced that phenomenon of how time changes everything. Everything becomes just a memory.

My mother is a lifelong student, but her core career throughout her life has been as a registered psychiatric nurse with a special focus on forensic psychology. She has worked in forensic wards of the mental health units at hospitals across Canada, with patients who have been deemed a danger to themselves or to others. She's worked in prisons, specifically women's prisons, with women who had addiction issues. She does a lot of really hard-core frontline emotional and mental intervention with our people.

When she first got her degree as a registered psychiatric nurse, my mom worked in the geriatrics ward of the sprawling Brandon Mental Health Centre, taking care of people with dementia. I remember as a little kid visiting my mom up in the hospital. She would bring me there because the old people loved being around little children and a lot of their families didn't visit them. Through my mom's activities and her work, I was always interacting with a lot of Elders, in unconventional ways. From a very young age, I was taught by my mom to take care of people because that's what she did for a living. I was taught from a young age to care about mental health, about people, about humanity.

When former prime minister Brian Mulroney reduced healthcare transfers, and provincial budgets across the country systematically dismantled mental health programs, the Brandon Mental Health Centre closed down. I often thought about what happened to all those old people, those Elders, who I would see at the Halloween party or the Christmas party at my mom's ward. Most people in state-funded mental health institutions got let go right onto the streets. That's why to this day, when you go to places like the Downtown Eastside in Vancouver or Higgins and Main in Winnipeg, a lot of the homeless people there actually have mental health issues. But there's no universal health care to cover their needs, and they don't have anybody helping them maintain their medication regimen. Often people with mental health issues who have no family support end up back on the street and sometimes self-medicating with illicit street drugs.

Before Roddy and my mom split for good, when I was six, Roddy got me a husky, which I named Sheba. I loved that dog. She was the most amazing dog. Roddy had found her on the side of the highway outside of the city. But she got sick very quickly. After a couple months she started shitting and pissing everywhere. She started having tremors. My mom wasn't around and Roddy wasn't around and I was a kid trying to take care of a dying dog. I remember trying to take Sheba for walks and she was so sick she couldn't even walk. She'd just lie down. I have always felt bad because I got angry at her. I remember whipping her with a stick and I regret that to this day.

I came home one day shortly after, and Sheba was gone. I said to my parents, "Where's Sheba? What'd you guys do with my dog?" They said that Sheba had to go to a farm. To this day I hope that Roddy put her down humanely but I'm pretty sure he just went back out and dropped her off on the highway again.

Roddy and my mom, during this period when they were trying to make it work, went to a parent-teacher interview in my kindergarten class at Linden Lanes. While we were there, I told my teacher, Ms. Gryer, and some parents, "When my mom gets mad at me, she grabs me by the braids and she bashes my head against the wall." I remember the look of horror on my mom's face. Roddy looked at me like: *You're gonna fucking get it, boy.*

When we got home, Roddy took his belt off and he was going to beat me, and my mom took his belt and said, "Nah, I'll do it." My mom took me into my room and told me, "You gotta scream like your life depends on it." She started whipping the bed and I started screaming. After she stopped, Roddy came into the bedroom and said, "Now I'm gonna inspect your ass." He pulled my pants down to see if there were belt marks. There weren't any marks, but he let it slide and he didn't beat me that day.

My cousins and I had a lot of friends from the cooperative housing in Central Park Winnipeg where we lived during the summer. It was a great time. Sometimes we would all get together and throw balloons off the balcony. This one time my great-grandfather, Edward Hart, was staying with us, us cousins were sitting on the balcony and throwing water balloons down and we hit a guy and he got so pissed off. He yelled up, "You little fucks!" shaking his fist at us. We were giving him the finger from the fifth floor. He called the cops and the cops showed up at our door. My auntie Isabel was out that evening. My great-grandfather answered the door.

The cops said, "Hey, we got a report there's some kids throwing water balloons off the balcony."

My great-grandfather said, "Oh yeah?" He was Mr. One Sentence, because he didn't speak much English. He spoke mostly Cree. He let the cops in. My great-grandfather said, "Was that you kids throwing water balloons off the balcony?"

We said, "No sir, no sir. It wasn't us. Nope, not at all. There's no water balloons here."

The cops said, "All right. Well, you better not because we're watching you. We're keeping an eye out. This is a real dangerous thing to do."

We said, "Yeah, we agree. We would never throw things off a five-storey balcony to hit pedestrians, sir."

So the cops left. Then our great-grandfather gave us all a look, shook his head, and went and had a smoke. We went through a second layer of anxiety, worrying if he was going to tell Isabel when she got home. The coolest thing about that moment is my great-grandfather didn't rat us out. When Auntie Isabel returned, she asked, "How were the kids?"

He said, "Good. Good. We had a nice time."

One day that summer that Roddy left for good, I went over to my friends' place on Evergreen Boulevard and they were watching George Romero's *Dawn of the Dead*, the one in a mall. My mom always said, "Don't watch scary movies. You're gonna have a nightmare." But it was one o'clock in the afternoon and I said to myself, *It's the daytime, so it's not going to be scary*. By that point my mom had started to date my German dad, Harry Müller, and he was spending the night. I came home after watching this zombie movie and I turned on every light in the house and I was banging on my mom's bedroom door, screaming, "Let me in! The zombies are gonna get me!" I could hear her laughing and saying, "Go to bed. The zombies aren't gonna get you. You shouldn't have watched that damn horror movie anyway. I told you you're gonna have nightmares." I was yelling, "No! They're gonna come and they're gonna eat me!" I was crying and snot was dribbling down my face and I was banging on the door. I could hear Harry laughing. I fell asleep with every light on, including the basement light, and, well, the zombies didn't get me.

My third father, Harry Müller, was a German soldier stationed at Shilo, the Canadian Armed Forces training base outside Brandon. At the time, Canada had a training contract with the German military. They would bring in nine-monthers, three-monthers, and three-weekers, whom they called gophers. German soldiers would come to the base in Brandon and they would train on the Leopard and Panther tanks. Harry was a heavy-duty mechanic who worked on those tanks.

A lot of the local Native women, my mom included, would go to the clubs—the Red Pepper Disco or Encounters—and date around, snag these three-weekers. The German soldiers all fetishized the Native women. They all wanted a Pocahontas. The Native women must have felt the same way about the Germans. My mom's sisters had a different German boyfriend every weekend. A whole generation of Native kids have German dads they never knew. My cousins' fathers all disappeared. But my mom and Harry stuck it out. For a while anyway.

Harry was a sweet guy. One day I asked if he would be my dad. He said he'd be honoured. Now my birth certificate says "Harry Müller" under "Father." I can get a German passport.

Of course Roddy did what he could to stop this new arrangement. He showed up at the house to beat the shit out of Harry, but Harry wasn't afraid. He was the size of the tanks he worked on. He stepped outside to have a word with Roddy, and a scuffle broke out. But my mom wasn't having it. She broke it up. She also punched Roddy in the face so hard a tooth came through his lip.

Looking back, I see that something must have broken in Roddy after that. He used to show up at school and talk to me through the chain-link fence. I remember his face, pixelated by the chain, asking, "How's it going, kid?" while the other kids played and yelled behind me. When Harry became my dad, Roddy showed up at court to relinquish any claim to visitation. He told the court he couldn't stand being around a Nazi. That's what he called my new dad. In the months before that, he would take me over to his apartment outside of the city. One time when I was there, I had scabs on my arm from having wiped out on my bike. He took a straight razor and he cut my scabs off my arm and put them in a box full of other scabs. Then he dumped alcohol all over my cut. I cried and he told me to be a man.

When I visited him Roddy at that apartment, he would make me read a book about Nazi Germany and the Holocaust. He would show me what Nazi Germany did to the Jewish people. Then he would say, "That's what Harry's people did. That's what your mom's new boyfriend is going to do to you. He's going to do to you what you see in this book." Whenever he picked me up, he'd say, "Is that Nazi inside fucking your mom?" So I didn't mind that the visits were going to end.

That's how the happiest part of my childhood began. It was great having a man around the house. Harry was a provider.

He'd had to return to Germany at the end of his tour, but he returned to Brandon as soon as he could, and soon he and my mom were married. At first he had to work at the Mohawk gas station, but he gradually qualified as a truck mechanic and was always taking courses to get this or that ticket. I remember what a big deal it was when he got his first set of Snap-on tools.

As a family, we went from the ghetto to the middle class. That was the first time I had ever lived in a single-family house. The little white kids had always seemed so rich to me, but now I was like them. My cousins could see the difference too. I could tell they resented my luxurious new lifestyle. Harry was always barbecuing, and my German oma was always sending me packages of German candy and clothes. Of course, German fashion was a little ahead of what people were wearing in Brandon at the time. My clothes made me look like I had just stepped out of the Capitol in *The Hunger Games*. But I thought I looked cool.

When I was eight or nine, we all flew over to Germany for Christmas to meet my oma and opa. I have strong memories of flying over the Atlantic, listening to Billy Joel on the plane's sound system, and landing in Frankfurt and feeling like the airport there was something out of *Star Wars*. I was a long way from the bus station in Winnipeg.

My grandparents lived in a beautiful four-storey house. They had a huge, gleaming piano and a cellar full of jars of preserves. I played chess almost every day with my German cousin, who didn't speak a word of English. Naturally I was in love with her by the end of the three weeks, and heartbroken to have to leave.

Across the street from the house was the little pub where Harry had tasted his first beer. He took me over one afternoon so I could taste mine. I had always been terrified of booze. It had always meant that something bad was going to happen. But no one was freaking out. No one was fighting or acting like sluts. It was a cool cultural moment for me. I felt grown up, and cosmopolitan, and I was there with Harry, who made sure everything was OK.

It was a beautiful Christmas. One evening, my opa took us all to the pool. We stopped along the way at a Christmas market for roasted chestnuts and waffles. The lights were just coming on, and a light snow was drifting down, and we were all dressed up. We were a happy family.

I thought it might last forever.

In grade 3, I was at a school called Meadows Elementary in Brandon and I believe my teacher's name was Miss Sherlock. For weeks my family and I had been preparing for the arrival of my oma and opa from Germany. We were going to do the National Lampoon–style family vacation and go to Disneyland. We were going to drive there in a big old-school early '80s station wagon that my dad Harry had borrowed from one of his German military buddies. My mother and I made a bed in the back and Oma and Opa would sit in the middle and Dad would be up in the front. It was going to be this huge excursion across the continent, through South Dakota, past what they used to call Devils Tower in Wyoming, through Yellowstone National Park and the Bay Area, and down the coastal highway of California till eventually we would end up in Anaheim and of course at Disneyland, and I could finally meet Mickey Mouse and Donald Duck and all those Walt Disney characters.

I bragged about this trip to all the other kids at school for weeks and weeks. The Friday came and I was walking around chest out, telling everybody: "You ain't going to see me for two weeks cuz I'll be gone." We left that day after school. We packed up a tent trailer and the station wagon and we took off to the border. The border crossing near the community of Brandon is fairly small. When we got to the border, it was pretty late and the lights were off and nobody was there. My dad was very much a newcomer and he didn't understand how militarized the Canada-US border was. He thought it was just like Europe where you could drive across the border with no consequence.

We were about thirty kilometres into North Dakota when US Border Patrol agents caught up with us and pulled us over with guns out. They arrested us and impounded our vehicle and our camper, neither of which belonged to us, and they made us walk with our luggage back to Canada. It was the first time I'd heard the term "illegal alien." Luckily there was a motel not far past the border where we were able to spend the night, and my dad called one of his friends to come and pick us all up the next day, which was a Saturday.

My oma and opa were pissed because we were trapped in Brandon, so we had to make up some shit to do. My dad said, "Let's go to Riding Mountain National Park, there's buffalo there." We went to Riding Mountain and we were setting up our afternoon beach site. Then my dad said, "Oh fuck!" and there was Oma, already topless and now flinging the bottom of her bikini off, buck-naked on a packed beach. My dad was chasing her with a towel, talking to her in German, saying, "Hey, it's not like that here, you can't do this, c'mon." She was slapping him away, saying, "Don't you talk to me like that, you little bastard."

I spent all that weekend crying to my mom and Harry that I just wanted to stay home for two weeks and not go to school. I felt the weight of having bragged to every single student at school, as well as the entire administration, that I was going to be in California for two weeks with my oma and opa. Monday morning came around and my mom, being who she is, told me I had to go to school and that I should just be honest and when you're honest, everything is OK. So I went to school. I could feel all the kids looking at me and whispering. Some of them taunted me, saying that I'd been lying, that I was never going to Disneyland in the first place. In class, I had my head down and was hiding my face. Miss Sherlock made me come up to the front of the class and she said, "Well, obviously you're not on your way to Disneyland, Clayton. So do you want to explain to us why you are here with us this morning?" I tried to explain what had happened from my grade 3 perspective, with my father who was a German citizen blowing through the Canada-US border at midnight without checking in with customs. I started to cry. "We got arrested because we were aliens." Most of the class laughed at me and my teacher put her arm around me and said, "You know, Clayton, you don't have to make up extravagant stories to fit in. You can just be yourself. Nobody's going to like you any less if you don't go to Disneyland. You don't have to lie about it to sound cool." Then she asked me to take my seat, and for the rest of my time there at Meadows Elementary, kids would tease me and say things like, "Why don't you go hang out with your friend Mickey Mouse instead of us?"

Eight or ten months after that failed trip, my oma and opa returned to Canada and we attempted another trip across the States—this time with success. By this point we had our own vehicle, a Jeep Cherokee. My dad got a Starcraft tent trailer that we towed behind the car. We were going to do a ten-state tour. Custer's Grave, Black Hills, the Seattle Needle, Mount Rushmore.

The really remarkable thing that I remember about that trip is that I must have masturbated in every single washroom across the ten states. We were all so amazed how cheap soda pop was down there, so we got cases of Dr Pepper that we were drinking non-stop and my dad cut me off from Dr Pepper, saying, "We can't be stopping six times an hour for you to go pee." The whole time I was laughing to myself because I knew what I was really doing in all those washrooms.

There was also this culturally awkward thing that was going on. In the trailer that we were sleeping in, there was just a thin curtain that clipped together with metal clips in between my bed and where my oma and opa would sleep, and every night they would get the trailer rocking and Oma would be moaning in Deutsch and Opa would be saying, "Ja, ja, it's good. Wunderbar." And I would be thinking: *What the heck?!* Then my mom in their bed on the other side of me, behind another thin curtain, would start laughing her head off. Thirteen days on the road and they did it every single night, like clockwork.

Every summer when we were living in Brandon, my mom would take me to Winnipeg, where I'd bounce back and forth between my cousins' place and my kokum's—that's my mother's mother, who liked to be called GiGi. The year I was eight she couldn't do the trip with me, and I was too young to ride the bus alone. One day one of my mom's good friends, Loni, was over and my mom was complaining, "I don't know how I'm going to get my kid over to Winnipeg for his summer trip. I can't put him on the bus alone." Loni said, "I'm going to Winnipeg. I'll bring your kid." I barely knew Loni. He was a Carib guy with a really thick Island accent. He was a very animated individual and in incredible physical shape, a powerful man. He'd come over and say, "Let's do push-ups, Clay." And he'd do push-ups and I'd join him. The thought of spending two hours driving to Winnipeg with him was intimidating.

The morning we were to leave, he rolled up in his Lincoln Continental. I got in the car and he was blasting Rick James on the eight-track. It was hella funky and I suddenly felt very cool. We set off. He was puffing big joints and Rick James was going on about being in love with Mary Jane, and how she was his main thing. I was sitting there on the big bench looking at him, and he was singing every word, puffing this big joint, laughing at me. We were driving down the centre of the Trans-Canada, one wheel in each lane, in this huge Lincoln, and he was talking about all kinds of stuff that as a young kid I didn't really comprehend: the smoke he was going to pick up, the beautiful women that he loved. Mostly talking to himself. That was the first time I heard the song "Electric Avenue" by Eddy Grant. Loni leaned over to me and said, "Yo, let's sing this shit." So we sang and it was glorious. Coming from Brandon, that drive made me understand that we were going to the big city. It put an incredible glamour on Winnipeg: We were listening to Eddy Grant and Rick James and it was the '80s and I was in a huge Lincoln with a Caribbean guy who was ripping joints. It was the most magical ride that I'd ever had in my young life. I felt like a king.

By the time I was eleven years old, my mom would put me on the Greyhound to do the two-hour trip to Winnipeg alone. I would never do that with my kids now, but things were different back then. I'd pull up to the bus depot in Winnipeg, which was a gathering place for many Natives in the city. There used to be a Salisbury House—an awesome old Winnipeg burger franchise— in the terminal that my mom would often take me to. I would arrive at the bus depot with my backpack and a fifty-dollar bill in my pocket that my mom had given me, and my cousins would be waiting: Rina and Starr, who were eleven and twelve, and Ed and Charlton, who were twelve and thirteen—no sign of my auntie or my uncle.

I'd say, "Hey cousins, let's roll. Let's go party." Kid party. So we'd go to the arcade on Portage Avenue. The big arcades were still a thing back then. It was before Nintendo. Atari was just starting to be a thing. These arcades were always full of down-town Indian children so I was very comfortable in them. All the popular music would be blasting from huge speakers mounted on the walls as though we were in a nightclub for kids. The sounds of the video games would compete with the music. We'd easily blow fifty bucks in seven hours, and then we'd roll to my cousins' apartment near Central Park downtown, and start watching TV and the parents would not even express an opinion.

In grade 4, at Flemming Elementary School, I did a paper on the human heart. We were supposed to draw and label the structure of the heart—the valves and the chambers and arteries. I wrote the paper after looking at my mother's medical textbooks. I drew the heart and I did it perfectly. It was so perfect that my teacher, Mr. Warren, called my mom and asked her if she had written my paper. I was really upset because he wasn't accusing me of plagiarizing, he was accusing me of having somebody else do my work. My mom told him, "No. He was up all freakin' night working on that paper. I sat with him but he did the work." I had even gone to the effort of changing the language from the medical textbook into my own words so I wouldn't be a plagiarizer.

After that experience, Mr. Warren treated me really well. He wanted to advance me into special classes for smart kids. I was labelled a gifted student. I was part of a weird little pilot program where I got to learn how to speed-read. They taught us how to read diagonally across the page.

The next year, grade 5, I got a teacher, Mr. Bird, who I didn't like so much. He was constantly picking on me. I was the only Brown boy in the class. He didn't like me.

How did I know that? How does anyone know someone doesn't like them? There's an undercurrent, a feeling you get as a Brown kid growing up when you know someone has a racial bias towards you. You can feel it in your gut. That's what the entire school year felt like. I was singled out a lot for failures when the whole class had stumbled, and was pinned down like a scientific specimen by Mr. Bird's dry, piercing humour. At the time, I didn't know this was racism. I just felt that this guy didn't like me, and I often got that feeling so many Native kids get when they are surrounded by white people: you feel dirty, like somehow you are ruining the party.

No kid can sustain his confidence in the face of snarkiness. I just gave up on school for the rest of that year. Sure enough, at the end of the year, I failed. I had been suspended a few times for fighting. At the beginning of the year, three boys had jumped me in the schoolyard over a girl that one of them had a crush on. We were all young kids and she and I were just friends. After the fight, though, I was the one who got punished and suspended, even though it was three on one. That was when I realized the system was rigged against me. One of these kids came from one of the wealthiest families in Brandon. The other was just another white kid who was one of the biggest bullies in my school, and the other was the only Black kid in my class. None of them got in trouble.

Over the next few months I hunted them down one by one, caught them when they were by themselves, and beat the living shit out of them. In the 1980s there was always that kid in the class and everyone would say: Don't fight that kid, he knows karate. One of the boys who had jumped me, Bryce, was the kid who knew karate. I caught Bryce alone in the washroom one day and he was the last one I had not gained revenge on. After putting his face in the urinal and beating his ass, I was surprised that he didn't rat on me to the teacher even though he had to spend the day covered in urine. We actually became best friends after that, and he went on to date the woman that he and his buddies had jumped me over.

The one thing I felt a lot of pride and joy about in grade 5 was my ability to serve and save lives as a member of the school safety patrol. I would come home after patrol and my mother would say, "How was your day, son? What did you do today?" And I would say to her: "Saved lives, Mom, saved lives." Because I was a patrol person and I helped kids get across the street safely.

One of the biggest school bullies, August, would always talk shit to me, but he never really bothered me until the day he said my mother was a whore. I took my patrol stick and beat August within an inch of his life on the steps of the school and I missed my patrol (as did August). The fight was very violent, and it escalated to the point where a janitor and a teacher had to pull me off August. I ended up punching the janitor and was restrained finally by the teacher. I got suspended for a week. August, being a white kid, did not get suspended.

As a student, I never really recovered. I never again had faith in the Western education system. I just gave up.

When I was in grade 7, my mom, and my sister Starina, and me moved to the town of Dawson Creek, in northern British

Columbia. Everyone seemed to be moving west in the 1980s in search of good-paying jobs, to Alberta to the oil patch or to British Columbia to the forests. My mother and my stepfather jumped on the bandwagon.

Harry got a job working as a mechanic in the logging industry on the coast and we lived apart from him for a winter. My mother got a job as a registered psychiatric nurse with the mental health unit at the Dawson Creek General Hospital, and then after a winter, she secured a job at the hospital in Terrace, were Harry had been living and working. Starting over was the only thing I knew after a lifetime of my mother moving me to new neighbourhoods, new homes, new schools when she couldn't make rent, or had to get a new job, or was trying to cope with other aspects of living in poverty.

I was going to the school called Tremblay. There weren't a lot of Native kids in that school, which was surprising considering the number of First Nations around Dawson Creek. One day I was called to the principal's office, although I wasn't a problem student. Or not yet. The principal had a series of questions for me, starting with: "Are you ashamed of being an Indian?"

I said, "Excuse me?"

"Are you ashamed of being Aboriginal?"

I said, "Are you asking other students these questions?"

He said, "No, no, I just want to talk to you. Being Aboriginal, do you feel inferior to other students?"

This principal probably had good intentions, in the same way that nuns who cut Indigenous children's hair off and beat them for speaking their language did. He likely didn't think of the consequences of singling me out and, I guess, trying to show solidarity by trying to get me to express his idea of what I was thinking. That's my guess, anyway, looking back. At the time, though, I figured I knew a racist jackass when I saw one. I was educated, and my mom was political, and I knew that pulling me into his office without my mom and asking me questions about my psychological stability and how confident I felt in this weird little town in northern British Columbia was not OK.

It was at that point that I started to realize that white folks are just as fucked as Native folks. Strengthened by the teachings of my mom, I said, "My mom's a registered psychiatric nurse. She's got a university degree in sociology. I live a pretty good life and I think you need to call her at work right now or I'm going to freak out. You need to ask her for permission before you ask me crazy questions like this." I had memorized the number at the hospital ward where she worked, because I would babysit my little sister every day after school and needed to know her number in case of emergency. I told him the number and he reluctantly called her. Before she arrived, I told the principal, "I'm the only kid in the school that's got a Nintendo Entertainment System." My mother, she really took to spoiling me because she was never home, she was always working. And of course I had been to Europe. So I knew Dawson Creek was a backwater.

My mom walked to the school from the hospital, which was not far away, in her nurse's outfit and read the riot act to the principal, saying, "How dare you ask my kid these questions!" Their conversation ended with him profusely apologizing for his inappropriate queries. I never did hear from him again. Years later, I heard that Tremblay burned down in the night, when no one was inside. I'm not going to say I was happy about it but I certainly wasn't sad.

After a short time in Dawson Creek, my mom, sister, and I moved to Terrace. Terrace was a mostly white logging town and I found it just as difficult to fit in as I had in Dawson.

Still, at that time, the Skeena River and all its tributaries were bursting with salmon, trout, and steelhead. There was incredible abundance. The old people would say, "You can run across the river on the backs of the salmon!" To get away from all the racism in Terrace, I would take off into the bush, and I would go fishing for trout. I spent a lot of time connecting with that salmon culture that our First Nations relatives in British Columbia hold so dear to their hearts and that is at the core of their culture. I knew where all the best fishing spots were and I would go by myself. I wasn't really afraid of anything in the bush because I had my dog Schnoof with me. I'd first met Schnoof when I visited my oma and opa in Germany. He was an amazing dog; they later shipped him to me in Canada. You couldn't leave Budweisers around because he would bite through the can, drink the whole thing, and get shitfaced.

I really didn't know how to deal with the racism I experienced and I didn't have anyone to guide me. My mom helped me in her way, but in many ways I felt I was completely on my own. Harry didn't speak English that well, and he didn't know how to coach me to deal with and confront in a healthy way the systems of oppression I was encountering in school and in society. He would say, "Oh, don't listen to that crap. You're a smart kid. Work hard! Play hard! That's it. Go to bed!" That's my dad, God bless him. But it wasn't enough and it wasn't what I needed.

I ended up being expelled from every junior high school in that town. I was kicked out of Skeena Junior so I went to the next junior high school in Thornhill, a community attached to Terrace, and the principal there expelled me on the last day of school. I had led a charge, a bunch of kids, and we had robbed the commission stand. We stole a bunch of packs of candy and beef jerky and we gave it out to all the students. Everyone was unpacking their lockers for the end of school and I was throwing around candy. It was a celebration.

There'd been eight of us. Only I got expelled. The principal walked me off the campus. He said, "You're fucking up your life." I shook his hand and said, "You don't have to worry about me." I wasn't even allowed to take the school bus home. I had to walk sixteen kilometres. Every day I lived in Terrace, I would look at myself in the mirror and say: "None of this is real. This is all fake. None of this has anything to do with you. You are really cool." Once I wasn't in school anymore, all the white kids wanted to hang out with me.

While we were in Terrace, my mom recognized that she needed to keep me busy to keep me out of trouble. When I was in my early teens, I qualified for youth nationals with the Terrace Bluebacks Swim Club as the fifth-fastest swimmer in my age group for the province. I was on the path to be an Olympic-level swimmer. I had a crew of friends in my junior high, and all of us matured physically very quickly. We would travel from town to town for volleyball, basketball, and other sports. We would win every tournament. We'd shatter records in track and field. I was even compelled to train on my own. I would run fifteen kilometres almost every other day up a famous hill in Terrace called Heartbreak Hill. I'd get up to the top of the hill, near the airport, where there was a gravel pit. I'd sprint up the gravel pit like I had wings. Gravel would be tumbling down and dust would be flying everywhere.

I'd placed a little shrine with candles and a picture of my girlfriend, Florence, at the top of the big pile of gravel. I'd get to the top and I would light the candles. Like a lot of young people I knew, Florence had a lot of issues. She was very antisocial, but she was the most beautiful woman I had ever seen at that point in my life. She was my first girlfriend in junior high, for two years, and she ripped my heart out of my body. It took me years and years to get over her.

What a head trip it was to be a young teenager and experiencing emotions and falling in love and having your heart broken and being exposed to everything you get exposed to when you're young, like drinking and smoking pot, especially in northern British Columbia. After my relationship with Florence ended, I quickly lost interest in the positive aspects of my life, and turned to partying. I became a skater, which was kind of the radical sect in the little town where I lived. I started to get into trouble.

I began to fall away from sports and school and began spiralling. By then, Starina, my little sister, had grown up. My mother took on a second daughter from my uncle Alec and my aunt Bernadette. So she had a lot on her plate.

And then she and Harry divorced.

By the time I was fifteen years old, I had racked up an incredible debt to Harry. Julie George was a beautiful and bright shining star. She was also my good friend Tyler's girlfriend and my best friend growing up. Julie and I would often talk on the phone so long we'd fall asleep talking. Those conversations cost me thousands and I would have to pay my father back every cent. (Eventually Julie ran away and came up to Terrace to see her boyfriend. He was a total dick to her and she ended up staying with me. We had a lovely visit, completely platonic. I persuaded her to go home and then we fell out of touch. It is not easy to fall in love with your friend's girlfriend.)

And of course my father was very upset with me for running up our phone bill and demanded I pay every cent back. Luckily, when the school year ended, I had an opportunity to go back to Pukatawagan to work under my uncle Alec, who is a fire chief with the northern firefighters. Firefighters make good money, and this was my chance to pay Harry back. Firefighting is big business up north. Many Natives fight forest fires professionally. My uncle's one of those people. So even though I was underage that summer I turned fifteen, he got me on the working crews.

My cousin Charlton came with me. There was a fire raging on a peninsula. We got helicoptered in and dropped off and we had to cut what's called a fire line across to keep the fire from jumping to the mainland. It was gruelling work. I got back to Pukatawagan after two weeks of firefighting in the bush. I had made quite a bit of money and bought a bunch of cigarettes— though I lost every single pack to the old-time firefighters late in the evening when we'd play poker. I had made enough money to pay my father back the money that I had racked up talking to Julie George on the phone, so I was beaming.

While I was in Puk, I ran into all of my cousins, Starr and Rina, Peter, and of course Charlton, who I worked with, all of whom I grew up with. Throughout our lives we had spent a lot of time together, both in Pukatawagan and on my great-grandparents' trapline. This was my first time going back to Puk as a young adult. At that point, I was a competitive racer in swimming and I raced in the Treaty Days swimming competitions in Puk and absolutely annihilated everybody and won a few hundred bucks. I also competed in the ten-mile run from Mile 99, where the train comes to our community, all the way into the core of the reserve. I came in fourth, so missed the cash prizes.

During that time, I developed a romantic interest in a local girl, Selena. She was the most beautiful woman in the community and I was burning up inside for her. Selena and I ended up dating, and one night she asked me to come by her house. Everybody knew that Selena and I were starting to hang out and it was local knowledge that, as the visiting city boy, I was due for a serious ass-kicking from the local boys. Pukatawagan is a notoriously hard place to grow up, very violent, and has on multiple occasions had the highest murder rate per capita in North America. I knew walking to Selena's on a Friday night would be dangerous, so I made a makeshift weapon out of a fork that I bent into a stabbing tool. As I walked to her house, in the span of one kilometre from my great-auntie Caroline's house to Selena's place, three different crews of young men jumped me and tried to stab me. I managed to stab my way through all the local crews trying to hunt me; basically, I stabbed my way to romance. When I got to Selena's house, she said, "Holy, why'd you take so long?" I said, "I had to stab my way through the barbarian hordes of Pukatawagan." And she had a little chuckle.

At the time, my brother Little Pete was working at the toxic waste site in our community. This was a PCB contamination site, and they had hired a lot of our community members to clean out the contaminated soil. I remember being very disturbed going to the site and seeing my brother down in the muddy pit without any protective gear on, no double-duct-taped heavy-duty rubber boots or containment gear that you would see anybody wearing in any kind of facility where you're cleaning toxic waste. I said to him, "Oh man, why don't you have any kind of safety gear on or respiratory breathing gear?" He said, "Oh no, it's OK. They give us these little patches and if it turns black it means you're absorbing too much PCBs." I remember thinking, *Fuck, that's real messed up*. Years later I would recognize that was a form of environmental racism: white multinational or Crown corporations creating a toxic waste site and then paying the local community to clean it up and not giving them the right safety gear. Pete has gone through some pretty rough times over the years, last I heard he was living in Pukatawagan. He is a father with many kids, but I have yet to make a relationship with my nephews and nieces.

One night my brother Little Pete, my cousin Charlton, and I all ended up getting tattooed. First, we stopped at the local bootlegger, who was my father's mother. It was the first time I had met my grandmother. She answered the door and yelled at me, "What do you want, a mickey or a twenty-sixer?" I was hurt. My brother Little Pete said to her in Cree, "This is my brother, your grandson." She hugged me and we bought two mickeys. After we left my grandmother's, I got an eight-ball tattooed on my shoulder from some guy who had a tattoo gun made from some kind of motor mechanism from a cassette deck. It got horribly infected. It's an ugly tattoo but I still have it.

I had become disillusioned with school and was getting into consistent arguments with teachers, especially social studies teachers, about what they were teaching about Canadian history. Why did the social studies books have only two pages about Indigenous Peoples? Why did the Native components of the social studies book in northern British Columbia, in Tsimshian territory, have profiles on Plains Indians? Everybody in my age bracket learned that Indians lived on the prairies in teepees and they ate pemmican, which was berries mashed with dried buffalo meat. Everybody learned that we migrated over the Bering Strait from Asia. Social studies is taught in bizarre little tidbits, as though Canada had not been a collection of Indigenous nations before colonization, Manifest Destiny, and the Doctrine of Discovery.

As a young person raised by a strong and very political Native woman, I would never be quiet if I witnessed injustice. I started to fist-fight with the white kids who would call me epithets they had probably heard from their parents. If you haven't lived up north, you may not know just how rough it can get. A fist fight is nothing. All it takes is a look, and you have to be ready to go.

I began to argue with teachers who didn't appreciate having me challenge them in front of the whole class. I would debate the curriculum they were teaching. I began to fight with school administrators who didn't appreciate my disagreeing with them when they said I should respect these teachers who are lying to youth about the true history of this country. I was angry and I started to get into trouble.

I knew I was spiralling. But I couldn't tell: Was the world a mess, or was I? Or was it both? Everything was going to shit. I knew I had to protect something precious, but I didn't know what it was. I knew there was something better than the drugs and the fighting, the anger and the stupidity, and I knew I was heading in the wrong direction, but I never lost sight of that beautiful thing, whatever it was. Every day, I would wake up and tell myself, *This is not real. I'm not in this situation. People don't*

really hate me this much just because I'm Native. I'm not really this
much of a loser. This is all only temporary.

But things would get much worse before they got better.

I was alone at home in Terrace when my cousin Rina called to tell
me that Starr had died, that she was gone. Starr had been killed in
a car accident by a drunk driver. I walked outside and then I ran. I
ran the entire night until the morning. I ran until I could not
breathe. At that time I was in the early years of my puberty, my
manhood. Then my cousin, whom I'd grown up with since I was a
little baby, who was like a sister to me, was suddenly snatched away.

I got really angry at Creator. I said fuck it to life.

I flew back to Brandon for Starr's funeral. It was awful.
You'd think my family would be immune to grief after a while.
That's not how it works. I had so little hope, I couldn't afford to
lose any more. There were so few people in the world who loved
me in spite of everything, who knew me inside and out. I couldn't
bear to lose one of them. My grief was raw and overpowering.

When I returned to Terrace after Starr's funeral, I came right
back into my problems at home. I really got into it with Harry. I
tried to kill him once. He drove away with an axe stuck in the
door of his car. That was grade 8. I wasn't thinking about grad-
uation, or high school. I really didn't give a shit.

My friend Tyler had moved out of Terrace to Prince Rupert.
Strange to think that I was still in swim club even as my life was
spiralling. At first I'd just see him at swim meets. But soon we
found other ways to hang out. We were drinking, doing drugs.
Selling joints at the ski hill. We had an ongoing war with another
gang of Native kids. That more or less counted as good clean fun
at that time, in that place.

Then Tyler's older brother Rory moved in. Rory was kind of
troubled. That's when Tyler got into stealing cars.

Prince Rupert, where Tyler was living, was about an hour-
and-a-half drive away. If I wanted to see him, I needed a way to

get there and back. Tyler showed me how. Back then, his whole thing was Toyota pickups. You can start one of those with a pair of barber scissors. From there we moved to stealing cars with a dent puller. First you pull out the door lock, then pull out the ignition, then stick it in the starting mechanism. I could boost a car and be down the road in a matter of seconds.

So I'd find a car, bounce to Rupert, then ditch it. I'd hang out with Tyler, then steal another car to go home. I did that for a year. My life was completely unstructured. I wasn't really going to school. No meaning. I was done with everything. I was done caring about consequences.

I got into mugging too. My buddies and I would wait outside a liquor store or drug house. We were carrying knives and machetes, and of course skateboards too. We'd jack whoever came out, take whatever they had, and go party.

It was awful. It was exhilarating. I would hit a deep depression and rely on adrenaline to get me out of it. When the high wore off, I'd be lower than ever.

I was angry. *Fuck everyone.* That's what I thought. *You're a dirty Indian. You're not Indian enough. You're a loser.*

Yeah? Fuck you.

I remember one day I walked out of school and there were Tyler and Rory and a couple of other guys sitting in a stolen van outside the school. It was a perfect fall day. The sun was shining. Tyler was running away to Vancouver. He was going to steal cars professionally.

I told him it was a bad idea. I told him to come stay with me until shit settled down. He was facing a lot of charges, his life was falling apart, and I knew my mom would let him stay with us. He was going through the same thing I was: we were realizing we were Native and the world was against us. It felt like it was us against the world.

Rory said, "Fuck this guy. He's a pussy."

Tyler said, "See you around."

The next day I got a call from a metalhead buddy of mine, Matt. He said he was sorry about the news.

I said, "What news?"

He said, "You haven't heard?" He said, "Bro, Tyler died in a car accident last night. I heard it on the radio."

Matt and I sat in a field and smoked a pile of dope.

A few days later the phone rang. It was Tyler. I started crying. It was Rory who'd died. And one other guy. Another dude was paralyzed. Tyler had just got out of the hospital. He was fine, except he had lost all his teeth. Tyler had been driving. He had fallen asleep at the wheel. When the van crashed, the steering wheel had splintered his mouth.

When Tyler got back to Terrace, we went and got fucked up together. We made a pact. With Rory dead, I promised to be his older brother from now on.

During that time, I got to know a kid named Leon, kind of a badass rich white kid. We hung out with an adopted Native kid and another guy who had just immigrated from Germany. He and I used to speak German together. We only hung out for a few weeks but it was Leon who got me into robbing houses. It was nothing big at first. One night I was staying over at Leon's, and he just said, "We're going to do this thing, come on. You have to get in on this." We were all in it more for the thrills than for cash.

But one night Leon talked us into lifting a collector's hockey card collection. Wayne Gretzky rookie cards, things like that. We got in and we got out. But I left fingerprints behind. We were all busted. My mom came down to the RCMP station with me. The cop who processed me was an auxiliary police officer. He was actually my therapist in his other job. My mom was furious. Of course. She was there to teach me a lesson, not to calm the waters. She said, "Just tell them you did it!"

So I did. I had faith in my mom telling me to admit my guilt and for the courts to give me a free ride, but they had other plans.

I had committed to my own demise. I got charged with break and enter. They gave me a court date for a year later and conditions— one of which was house arrest. I'd been living on my own. I had to go back and live with my mom. At the same time, my mom and Harry were getting a divorce. My mom and I ended up moving into a home for abused women. Harry was having issues with alcohol. He wasn't abusive but he was distant. And there was nowhere else we could go. We moved every three months or so, till we moved into a house on Pear Street. But by then I'd gotten expelled from the alternative junior high school—for smoking a cigarette inside. Because I wasn't in school or working, my mom kicked me out of the house.

Usually in our overcrowded homes on reserves or in the inner city, when Native men turn a certain age we get kicked out of a bedroom and put on the couch. Eventually we get kicked off Mom's couch because usually there are other transient men coming in who have relationships with Mom and there's no room for young bucks. A lot of young Native males end up getting kicked out because single moms can't give them what they need and can't control them. We quickly learn how to be comfortable sleeping on Granny's couch or Auntie's couch. So when I dropped out of school, I was on my own. Crashing with friends, couch-surfing, staying with my aunties Rhona and Kathy, or my grandmother, or friends. I was stealing things to get by, selling drugs on the side.

Everyone else's lives seemed so easy. I didn't feel as though others were going through the same thing as I was. They didn't have my grief. They didn't have my anger. Their concerns just felt childish to me. Soon, though, I began to have real, adult problems. Looking back, I am surprised at how fast things could change. One day I was swimming and hanging out at school.

Then, after Starr died, I found myself inhabiting a completely different world.

Tyler and me, our lives became dark. The world was too fucked up, and we completely closed ourselves off from it. Closed off from school, from our parents. We veered back and forth between Terrace and Prince Rupert, stealing cars, playing smash-up derby, driving them off cliffs. We lurched between numbness and exhilaration.

Tyler was more reckless than I was. He was more haunted, because he had killed his brother. He always wanted to fight. And there was always someone willing to fight him.

This went on for almost a year. We did a few B&Es, smashed a lot of windows, and stole a lot of booze. But not much that would count as robbery. Until we heard about a safe with gold bars in it. We broke in and pried the safe open with a car jack. Not only were there gold bars, there was cash—and gold *teeth*. That freaked us out. Who keeps gold teeth in a safe?

I was on a roll. That same week, I broke into my next-door neighbour's. He was a cop. All I got was some booze. And I got caught. Fingerprints again.

I was told that I was under house arrest for this recent B&E, even though I was already under house arrest for the last one. I was still waiting for that trial. I couldn't go anywhere except school. And I wasn't going there anyway. But my mom had decided to move back to Winnipeg. She wanted to go back home now that she and Harry had split. The province of BC required that I have a legal guardian. So I went with her and switched my existing probation standards to Manitoba.

My behaviour didn't improve when my mom and I moved back to Manitoba. Me and Tyler had a similar experience of our families having landed in BC but still being anchored in Manitoba. His father lived in Manitoba and was still very much a part of his life, so when I returned to Winnipeg with my mom, Tyler and I would often cross paths. One time when Tyler was passing through Winnipeg, he and I and another buddy stole a car and drove to Brandon to pick up some of Tyler's stuff from his dad's place. We ended up in a high-speed car chase and crashed right into a house. The cops were on the

scene immediately, with sirens and dogs and the whole appara-
tus. Tyler was caught, but my buddy and I managed to slip
away. We lay low for a bit, then my buddy and I decided to
hitchhike back to Winnipeg before we got caught. Remember,
we were just kids. We were terrified, and the adrenaline was
kicking our asses. We were standing on the side of the highway,
on the edge of a grain field, when my buddy just collapsed onto
the gravel.

At that moment, a cop car approached, and nothing I could
do would wake my buddy up.

"You guys OK?" the cop asked.

I said yes.

"Does your friend there need a lift?"

It was kind of hard to say no. So I got him into the car and
piled in beside him.

When the cop shut his door, he picked up his radio and said,
"I got 'em." He took us to jail. I stayed in jail the whole weekend.
Tyler's dad somehow got me released. He was so fucking angry.
He drove me to the Greyhound station and said "You are never
to see my son again." Then he put me on a bus to Winnipeg.

When my court date for my first B&E came up, I went back to
Terrace. My friends' lawyers used my confession as a way of getting their clients off. They claimed that I was the ringleader, that
I had led these kids astray. They didn't get probation. They all
got slaps on the wrist, and I had expected to get a slap on the wrist
too—probation, maybe a fine. But I was made an example of, I
believe because I was the only Native in the crew. I'll never forget
being in the courtroom and hearing the judge say, "You get four
months for the crime that you committed." Florence was there.
My buddy had his arm around her. They were dating.

I was sixteen and didn't know how it worked—I thought
I'd have a chance to go blow off some steam with some friends
and then check into jail. But no, they take your ass into custody

right there in the courtroom. They take you in the back, they take all your personal effects, your belt, your shoelaces, and they put them into a plastic bag and you don't see that shit until you get out.

On my way to juvie in Prince George, they had me in a van with the adult prisoners who were going to the adult jail. These old Native guys, serving life on the installment plan, were giving me advice on how to survive in juvie. As soon as the van started rolling, one old guy said, "Hey little man, this your first bit?" I didn't like the idea of having more than one. Another guy offered me cigarettes, advising me that they were like gold inside. "Here, take them," he said. "Shove them up your butt or they'll take them away from you."

I didn't like the sound of that either. I didn't shove them up my butt. The guards took them away when they took away my clothes. It seemed like a waste of that old guy's generosity.

One guy said, "Listen. The number one thing you got to do—the number one thing you gotta do—as soon as you get in there, you find the toughest guy and he's gonna have a lieutenant. And his lieutenant is gonna be sitting right beside him. You walk up to that guy and you friggin' bop him right in the face. Then nobody will ever fuck with you. They'll think you're crazy." I said, "OK. OK, I'll do that."

When I got into the TV room, where all the other inmates were, I could feel the eyes on me. Everyone was sizing me up. I was sizing them up, looking for the leader. I spotted him easily. A huge guy, with another muscled-up redhead dude beside him. That was the lieutenant. Christ. I knew it was now or never.

I grabbed a chair and I busted it over the lieutenant's head. Then I kicked him in the face. He was tough, though. We were punching and rolling on the floor until the officers arrived, and then we got in a fight and the guards broke it up. While I was pinned, that fucker grabbed my dick and balls and pulled as hard as he could.

I was locked up for twenty-four hours for being the instigator, but no one fucked with me after that in the Prince George Youth Custody Centre.

My months in juvie taught me strength through terrible loneliness. You're just by yourself. I wanted my mom so badly I would cry at night in my little room, thinking about her. I hadn't seen her in months. My baby brother Marco was born while I was in juvie. I didn't get to see him when he was born. I turned seventeen in there and I didn't have anybody with me.

My mom raised me on three leaders. She would read me quotes from Dr. Martin Luther King Jr., Malcolm X, and Chief Dan George. When I was a kid, my mom gave me a copy of Malcolm X's autobiography. I found a tattered copy in the library in juvie, and I held on to that book. I must have read it thirty times. It made me feel that my mom was with me, even though it was too far for her to come and visit.

When I went into juvie I was fairly manic. I was a wreck. I was withdrawing from all the booze and drugs I'd been used to. I couldn't even have cigarettes. Just thinking about Florence cheating on me would send me over the edge.

So they put me on a bunch of antipsychotic drugs to calm me down because I wasn't sleeping. Those drugs caused me to gain a lot of weight. I went from 150 pounds when I went in to 230 pounds when I got out four months later. When I went into jail I had a long skater haircut, like a bob to my shoulders and shaved underneath. I completely shaved my head while I was in jail. My mom didn't recognize me when I came out.

In juvie, I formed a pipe dream that I was going to get out early for good behaviour. I conformed to the system. I made a decision to pass grade 9. I got a job in the kitchen. I made it as far as you could as a model prisoner, and had all kinds of recommendations in my file. But I struggled to keep my humanity because people treated each other so horribly inside.

Jail didn't reform me. It politicized me and made me sharper. I never went back to jail, although I did some bad things. One of the biggest lessons I learned while I was in juvie was how rigged the system is against Native people. Most of the guards in juvie were white guys, and they all had their favourite white prisoners that they would lend favours to so that the white kids would keep all the Native kids in line. There was a crew of white guys in there that were real big and real bullish and they'd pick on the little Native kids and do disgusting borderline rapey things to them. They'd grab their junk. They'd stuff shit up their asses. The corrections guards would perpetuate a culture of not ratting.

I was a big boy and I had been living on my own for a couple of years already by the time I went to juvie. I was basically a man. But many of these little Indian kids were just babies getting terrorized by the other kids and terrorized by the corrections officers. I felt terrible about it, but for most of my time in juvie I didn't do anything about it. I didn't put myself at risk because of my dream of getting out early.

The irony was that in jail I finally went to school. I did my grade 7 and 8 in one month. Told the teacher, "Just give me the tests."

Because of my good behaviour, I was transferred out of the closed custody unit after a month and sent to a youth custody centre called High Valley Camp, in Logan Lake, BC, near Kamloops. Thus I began my journey of seeing the province of British Columbia through jail, on BC taxpayers' dollars. High Valley Camp sounded exciting. You stayed in little cabins. You got your own kitchen in your cabin where you could have snacks. But it was actually a work camp. They would contract us out to the cattle ranchers around the region.

During the month and a half that I spent at Logan Lake, I got to be really intimate with this thing they call a post pounder, which is a big cylinder you put on a post to pound the post into the ground. We had to build cattle fences all across the mountains and then we had to unwind bales of barbed wire and attach the wire to make cattle fences. Around Kamloops is semi-arid. It was forty degrees on the side of those mountains on Logan Lake, and because High Valley was a co-ed facility, we weren't allowed to work with our shirts off. It was brutal work.

Again through good behaviour, I was able to get a job working in the laundry facility in High Valley Camp. So I had all the nice sweatpants and all the nice sweatshirts. I looked cool. I had a little racket going when I was in there. I would hook people up with nice clothes for stuff from the canteen, chips and candy or shaving cream, or extra food from the kitchen.

Nobody fucked with me, except one guy. He was like six-five, built like Conan the Barbarian. He was nineteen years old and he'd burned his school down. I don't remember his name but I remember thinking: *What the fuck are you doing in here? You're a full-grown man.* He used to go around and mess with everybody. We had a showdown, him and me.

I went to the gym to play dodge ball. When I saw him I smoked him in the face. He was talking some shit to me and I chucked a ball at his head and I hit him right in the face. He said he knew karate. Everywhere I go there's always the karate guy and it's like: *Don't fuck with him, he knows karate.* I got in his face and said, "Whatever, man. Use your karate then. Let's see what you can do." But the fight was broken up and both of us got put on marmot duty.

Marmots are big rodents, like beavers without a beaver tail. Farmers hate marmots because they dig holes in the fields and the cows step in these holes and their leg breaks and then they have to be put down. Every morning, you'd hear the corrections officers out in the fields shooting the marmots. There would be thousands of them. Those dead marmots would sit out there all day, baking in the sun, bloated with gas. In the afternoon the corrections officers would send out the kids who were acting badly to go collect the marmots. You had to collect them and then sit in the back of the pickup truck with a pile of dead bloated marmots.

When Conan the Barbarian and I were put on marmot duty, we were riding around in the truck with a guy and a girl who wanted to snag. The guy said, "Hey, hey, Thomas-Müller, sit over there, block the window." So I sat there on one side of the truck and blocked the window and they got the Conan guy to block the window on the other side of the truck and the dead marmots were piled so high between us so that the corrections officers driving the truck couldn't see past them. Then this guy and girl started fucking on top of the dead marmots. At that point, I thought, *What did I get myself into?* After we watched those kids fucking on the dead marmots, Conan the Barbarian and I never fought again. We kind of laughed about it and actually became friends. Any time tension started to rise between us, the ridiculous image of nasty sex on top of a heap of dead animals would make us laugh and defuse the tension.

I got selected through my good behaviour to go to a John Howard Society life skills program, in the community of Campbell River on Vancouver Island. It was amazing because they let you wear your street clothes. I lived in a cabin. There was a swimming pool and an obstacle course built way up in the trees. We zip-lined through these huge trees and then we did it blindfolded.

Being there was one of the greatest tests of my life. For my seventeenth birthday, some of the white boys peer-pressured my roommate, a young Native guy, to pick a fist fight with me in the gym. It really sucked because I didn't want to fight him. I tried talking to them. I said, "Guys, why you gotta be like this? We're in paradise. We got it going on here. We're living in the fucking mountains on Vancouver Island and we got a swimming pool. We're eating good food. Why would we fight? Why would we want to sacrifice this opportunity and get sent back to the shithouse?" Those guys weren't having it. So I had to fight my roommate. I beat his ass up and then those boys all tried to jump me. They picked up some bars that you weight-lift with. But I was fast. I was able to grab a bar and I fought my way out of the weight room and I just went to bed. My body was bruised and my adrenaline crashed.

When I woke up in the morning, my roommate had put a wooden ball in a sock and left it right beside my head, kind of like a message: *I could have killed you in your sleep.* I talked to him the next day and I said, "I don't know why all of a sudden you and me we got to be enemies because of these fucking white guys. I didn't want to fight you. We should have jumped those fucking white guys." And he just cried.

Eventually, my good behaviour got me into a halfway house. I could leave the premises, go to the store, although I wasn't allowed to smoke and had to keep receipts to show how I spent the allowance they gave. But it was cool. I was almost out. When I was in there, the group home supervisor was a Cree woman from The Pas, Opaskwayak Cree Nation—the sister community to my First Nation, Pukatawagan. She was a beautiful Cree woman, very stoic, very strong. I thought, *Right on, man. I'm living on Easy Street here and I got a mother figure that's going to take care of me. Life's looking up.* I'll never forget her response when she asked me who my dad was. When I said, "My dad's Peter Sinclair Sr.," a shadow fell over her face. I realized that at some point my dad had snagged with that woman or one of her sisters and broken her heart, or broken a sister's heart, and now I was going to pay for the sins of my father, because this woman had the keys to my freedom.

A couple weeks went by and there were two little Native kids who got sent to the halfway house. I don't know what I was thinking, but I told them, "Hey, go buy some smokes, guys, with your allowance." I didn't think they were actually going to go and buy smokes, but they did, and they didn't have a receipt for their allowance. That woman had a nose like a wolf, so when they smelled of cigarettes, she told those boys, "I'm going to send you back to the big house." They were crying and I told her, "Take it easy on these little boys. You don't have to do that. I bullied them. I told them to go buy cigarettes. They did it for me. Don't send them back to the big house." She didn't care. She sent all of us back.

I was shocked. After dealing with so many brutal fellow inmates, so many corrections officers who were bullying kids and using their power over the majority of Native kids who were locked up, to have a Native sister send me back to the Prince George Youth Custody Centre, after months of good behaviour, I just thought: *You know what? Fuck it. I'm not going to put up with being terrorized or seeing little Indian kids get terrorized by racist fucktards or racist corrections officers with fantasies that they are working in a maximum security prison.*

Imagine my surprise when I rolled back into Prince George and there was an old buddy of mine, Cohen. Cohen was a crazy Indian from Vancouver Island whom I had met briefly in High Valley Camp. Cohen had been shot. He had been stabbed. He had been run over. The fucking guy was tough as nails. We had become friends at Logan Lake. But then he stabbed some kid in the head with a fork and got sent up to Prince George to closed custody.

Upon my arrival back to PGYCC, Cohen and I talked at great length and devised a strategy to deal with the white bullies in our unit. We caucused with all the little Native kids in the unit and we said, "Fuck these guys who are making you do stuff for them, taking your treats, terrorizing you." We decided that if the corrections officers weren't going to protect these little Native kids, then we were going to do something about it. We got organized and we were powerful. One day, I walked into the TV room and I sat down in the toughest guy's chair. There was one armchair and all the rest were plastic chairs, and this tough guy would always take the armchair. He was the boss of the unit. I sat down in his chair and he came up to me and he said, "Hey Thomas-Müller, you're in my chair. It's time for my show." I said, "Fuck you. It's my chair now. This chair's not yours anymore." He couldn't say anything, because all of a sudden my bro Cohen was there—and everybody knew that

Cohen would stab your ass if you fucked around. So the tough guy just said, "You gonna regret this, Thomas-Müller. You gonna regret this." I said, "No. I'm not going to regret this." It was funny because I had had run-ins with this guy and his right-hand man, a fellow red-headed bully I fought when I had first got into juvie.

The cool thing about it was that once we had decided that we were going to band together and support one another, there was peace. Even the white guys had peace. There was no agitation. The corrections officers were upset because there was peace. It was completely ass-backwards to me. I was really adamant that we weren't going to do anything to provoke violence, that we didn't need to lose our humanity. I had conformed in juvie in an attempt to get released early for good behaviour. Then in my last month of juvie, I enjoyed a level of peace by not conforming—by organizing with the Native base in the youth detention facility. We were powerful in that moment.

When I finally left, I remember the looks on some of those kids' faces. I knew that they were going to get it after I left and I would have no way of knowing what happened to any of them.

When I got out of juvenile detention at seventeen, my third father, Harry Müller, was working in a logging camp in Haida Gwaii and my mother was in Winnipeg. I was still a minor, and they had no one to release me to. So the Province of British Columbia put me on a Greyhound one-way to Winnipeg. I moved in with my mom and tried to get my life back in order.

I went to school and I was actually the lead actor in the Shakespeare production—I was an Indian Macbeth. Unfortunately I never got to act in the play because I was expelled by Christmas for dealing drugs. I'd been selling cannabis oil that I kept in syringes in a Bible in my locker. My mom said, "No job? Not going to school? You can't stay with me." I said, "See ya!" I liked to take the long road when I was a boy.

I had friends so I couch-surfed, but there were a lot of nights that I didn't find a couch. It got to the point where I was digging in the garbage for food, sleeping in heated bus shacks. I'd walk the streets all night and quite often I'd come to the legislative grounds and cruise around and feel safe because it was so beautiful and not as rugged as other parts of the city.

One January night in 1995, I was really hungry and destitute. It was freezing and I had nowhere to go. I was walking around the legislative grounds and came to a payphone. I decided to call my biological father, Peter Sinclair Sr., who lived back home on our reserve. I didn't know what else to do or where to go. I called directory and said, "Do you have a Peter Sinclair Sr. registered in Pukatawagan First Nation?" I didn't even have a quarter to call my dad, so I called him collect. He accepted the charges.

"Hey Dad, how's it going?"

"Oh. Not bad. How are you doing?"

"Well, you know, I'm not doing so good. Actually, I'm homeless right now. I'm having a really hard time. Look, I've never asked you for anything before but I sure could use some help."

He was quiet for a little bit. "Well, my boy, I'm not going to send you any money but if you really want to work, I can get you some work."

"Yes. Absolutely. Thank you."

"I'm going to give you a phone number. Call that phone number and everything's going to be OK."

"All right. Thanks, Dad. Ekosi."

"Ekosi," he said, and he hung up.

I called the number and heard "Hello." Right away I knew it was my older brother Johnny. We'd been close before I went to juvie. I'd spent a couple weeks with him in Winnipeg after I fought forest fires back home on our rez and had a bit of money in my pocket. When I went to British Columbia to face my charges, I thought I'd get probation and come right back and hang out with him. But the courts had another plan for me, so my brother and I had lost touch.

"Ah. Shit, Clay," he said. "Holy cow. Where the fuck did you end up going, man? I thought we were supposed to go check out Pink Floyd. I had tickets and everything. Where the fuck were you? Holy shit, jail, eh? Well, where are you now?"

I said, "Yo man, I'm down on the legislative grounds. At a payphone on Broadway."

He picked me up and we went to Ken's Restaurant, a twenty-four-hour Chinese restaurant, and he got me caught up on what my brothers and uncles were up to. Many of them were in positions of leadership in the infamous Manitoba Warriors, one of the largest Native criminal organizations in the country. It had thousands of members.

The Warriors had started off as a beautiful vision of my uncle Brian: a job-creation opportunity for convicts who had done time and could now work as security guards at pow wows and other Aboriginal events. They explicitly aimed to provide members a sense of Native identity and culture and to offer safety from other gangs and violence that Native people often have to deal with. But it quickly spiralled into something darker. I guess that if you assemble a bunch of guys who are good at using the threat of physical violence to get what they want, you shouldn't be surprised if they start using their muscle in ways you hadn't originally intended. Muscle is like that.

It wasn't long before the Warriors were dealing drugs and running prostitutes. If you were going to do those things, you had to answer to the Hells Angels. But soon the Angels were answering to the Warriors. The Warriors were the only gang capable of rolling up the world's most famous biker gang. That's the kind of people the Warriors were. You didn't fuck with the Warriors.

My brother John introduced me to my uncle Brian, who by that point was the president of the Manitoba Warriors. John told Uncle Brian, "This is my little brother Clay and he wants to work, so you should hook him up with that gig." The "gig" was managing a drug house on Furby Street.

My uncle Brian lived upstairs in the duplex and I lived downstairs. I became close with his daughter and his two sons. Brian liked to keep his eyes on things and managed all the Warriors' business. All I had to do was serve up people at the back door: homies coming in and re-upping to sell grams in Central Park, or established members of the Native community coming to get their treats to go clubbing. All kinds of people would come to the door, at all hours, with TVs, diapers, baby formula, bricks of cheese, fucking steaks. Anything for a fix. I got sixty bucks a night just for my time and then I would get preferential price points for the acquisition of things I wanted to move on the side. Of course I had my own hustles on the side. Everybody had their own hustles. I moved a little ecstasy and cocaine on the rave scene to keep my own party going.

The summer I turned eighteen, I thought this was the sweetest gig ever. I could have all the weed I wanted. I could watch TV all day. It was every teenager's dream job. For a short time I felt like I was important, like I mattered. Obviously, gang culture has a real appeal to young men. They love being part of something, love feeling they've found a shortcut to power and success. Also, it's no accident they usually form along ethnic lines—there is a strong sense of "tribal" solidarity. It's dangerous, and stressful, but you hold your head high. You swagger.

My life had purpose again, for the first time in a long time.

I never really had the chance to grow up with my brother John. I had met him as a little kid on the bullet to Pukatawagan, the train between The Pas and Puk, and I'd spent a summer with him in Winnipeg when I was fifteen, before juvie. I'd always wanted more of a relationship with him. Throughout my teenage years, I had idolized my big brothers. John was the king of Winnipeg, a legend. Although he smoked dope, he never did coke, he never drank, and he never smoked cigarettes, and I was always impressed by that discipline. And he was a revolutionary.

In his youth, he had the nickname Johnny Treaty because he was always talking about treaty rights.

My other brother Alan would come around sometimes. Al was in and out of jail his whole life. He had served a life sentence for murdering his best friend over a mickey of alcohol. He and my other brother Little Pete were quintessential Indian gangsters. They drove all the fancy cars. They had long hair. Beautiful women would hang around with them. Everybody respected them. Nobody ever challenged them. Nobody could touch them, so suddenly nobody could touch me. At the time, I found that kind of respect, that kind of power, really appealing.

But that power comes at a hideous cost. I saw a lot of violence, a lot of really intense man-on-man violence and a tremendous amount of violence against women. I recall having to wash the blood off my brother's car after they'd return from collecting debt. Quite often, there would be meetings in the drug house I managed and lived in. All the high-ranking individuals who participated in the gang, my brothers included, would gather to conduct business, including disciplinary procedures over members who had done shit that was against the rules. I would have to watch my uncle Brian and brother John disciplining other uncles over making deals that weren't allowed to be made or were made outside of the family.

Johnny had a white Thunderbird (which may have belonged to my uncle Brian) with blue-tinted windows and a white leather interior. It was an Indian gangster car, a real G-car. It roared when it started. One day, my brother Johnny and I got out of his Thunderbird and were walking up the steps to the drug house. A woman in the house right next to ours jumped out of the second-storey window, screaming, and she rolled onto the roof. She was going to fall off so I came underneath and tried to catch her but she fell right through my arms and hit the ground. She was lying there, out cold, naked except for her underwear. A needle was sticking out of her arm. I looked at my brother John and my uncle Brian and I said, "What the fuck! We gotta do something! We gotta call an ambulance. We gotta help her." Uncle Brian said, "Get in the fucking house, man. Never mind that girl." As I was going up the steps, she jumped up and started running down the sidewalk. But she'd broken her leg in the fall. She was in her underwear, her shinbone protruding out of her skin, the rig still sticking out of her arm, running down the street.

I didn't realize until later how dangerous that whole time was. I could have gotten killed at any moment. I could have gotten beat down. There were a lot of people around my brothers who didn't like me, who thought I was a spoiled little shit. I heard stories about people who said that they were going to get me, and then my brothers got them first—and then they didn't get anybody. But one wrong statement, one wrong move, and one of these guys could have easily taken me out, big brother John or not.

I've grown into a big guy, but when I was working for the Manitoba Warriors, I was a buck fifty. Lean. The men I was hanging out with in the Warriors were two- and three-hundred-pound six-foot-plus Indians. Arms as big as my thighs. They'd done prison time and spent time building muscle. The thickness of their chests, the thickness of their legs and arms and heads, was impossible to me. They were like gladiators. Everybody was always trying to be tough and front on each other.

One time I was in the drug house with my brother and one of those big Indians, a guy named Big Mike. They brought in a sister, a young woman. I remember thinking that she was very attractive. Then they brought in some nasty old guy who had just gotten off the Greyhound from up north. Big Mike said to me, "Yo. We need your room for a while, homie." I said, "Fuck that." John said, "Don't go against Big Mike." So the young woman went in the room with this guy. I guess she provided him with services. It bothered me deeply.

Another time, a woman I was dating was sleeping at my house. It was early in the morning and Big Mike started teasing me. He said he was going to go into my bedroom and check out my cute girlfriend. I told him flat out, "Don't fuck around. You're in my house." He came at me—and I saw that the veil of safety around me was very thin. My brother John, who held the rank of a captain in the Manitoba Warriors, looked at Big Mike and said, "Leave the kid alone. Can't you see you're fucking upsetting him? Don't fuck around." Big Mike looked at my brother. And then he gave me this look like he was going to fucking kill me for talking shit to him. But I didn't flinch, even though he could have completely slapped me around. At that moment I knew I couldn't protect the woman I was dating, who was asleep in my bedroom. I knew I couldn't protect the people around me.

A couple of months later, Johnny came into my house as he always did, with his coffees. He'd buy himself four extra-large coffees from Robin's Donuts—double sugar, double cream—and he'd have a bag of six doughnuts. He was known as Johnny Bag of Doughnuts. He would sit in my house and roll impossibly perfect joints. We'd smoke the joints and philosophize and talk politics.

I always knew when John was being serious, when I needed to listen to him, because the rest of the time we were always shit-talking each other the way brothers do. That day, he came in and sat down and said, "Clay, I want to talk to you about something. I've always had respect for you. I've always treated you like a man. But this one time I'm going to treat you like my little brother. I'm going to tell you something and you're going to listen to me, because I'm your big brother and that's protocol. This is the only time I'll ever do that."

I said, "What the hell? What's going on?"

He said, "Yo man, I've been at this game for a long time and I know when the heat is going to come down, and the heat's coming down. I can sense it. I don't want this life. I'm a simple man. I want to have a wife, I want to have children, and I want to do what our father did when he was young and healthy. I'm going back to Pukatawagan. I'm gonna hunt moose. I'm gonna shoot duck. I'm gonna fish. I'm gonna get married and have kids and I'm never gonna come back to the city."

He said, "You are way too fucking smart to be wasting your time with all these losers. All these guys are going to end up dead. They are going to end up in jail and you have too much brains to waste your time like this. So listen to me. I want you to move out of here, tomorrow. I want you to have nothing to do with these guys anymore. I want you to disassociate yourself from the gang. I don't want you to be affiliated. Go do something with your life. Go to school. Do something."

I got mad at him. I told him, "Who the hell d'you think you are, man? Don't come to my house trying to tell me what to do!"

He sat there and listened to me. He was really humble and then he said, "I'll repeat myself. I've always respected you. But I'm your big brother and this is the one time I need you to listen to me. The heat's coming down and it's gonna get bad."

He got up and left. He went back to Pukatawagan, and he shacked up. He's separated now, but he has five kids. He hunts moose and he fishes commercially. He runs a pizza and chip shop called Mīciso, where the whole rez comes and buys pizza and fish. I always admired John for his choice to commit to a life in the bush. I'm happy for my nephews and nieces that he abandoned gang life and that he gave all his time to being a father.

At the same time, I had started dating a woman, Koren, and she really wasn't into the Manitoba Warriors. She said that I had too much sense to be doing that sort of thing and that I wasn't putting my skills to good use. She also expressed that my lifestyle choices were quite stressful. She didn't want to date a guy living that kind of high-risk lifestyle. She's Mennonite, and while her background isn't affluent, it is privileged. She always had what she needed. Her father and mother are very principled people. They both worked hard their whole life to get a house in Whyte Ridge, a development on the outskirts of Winnipeg. She told me flat out, "Dude, don't end up like your uncles and your brothers. If you don't get some ambition, I'm going to have to terminate this relationship."

So I listened to Koren and my brother. I moved out of the drug house. I talked with my uncle Brian, who was real sweet about it. He said, "OK, you want to go to school and make a life for yourself in that way. I can respect that. Go do your thing. I'll figure it out." The Manitoba Warriors hired some other young Native guy to run that house on Furby Street.

My experience with gang culture in the city was very different than that of the average young Native who gets involved in gang life. I never had to prove myself to anybody. I was quickly put into a position of privilege and comfort. Because of my family connections, I didn't have to face any kind of recruitment ceremony or initiation. Because of my family's street cred, I never had to go through what everybody else goes through when they leave a gang. You get jumped out, maimed for life if they don't kill you.

A couple of weeks after I left, the government of Canada brought in new anti-gang legislation. It was a major piece of legislation in the mid-'90s that amended the Criminal Code to give special arresting and prosecuting powers to the Crown and police forces in order to target criminal organizations. It was primarily designed to take down organized crime in Montreal—the Hells Angels and the violent biker wars, where bombings and all kinds of atrocities occurred—but they tested the legislation through a massive operation in Winnipeg that targeted the Manitoba Warriors. At the time, there was a lot of conversation in the media about how the fastest-growing sector of gangs in Canada was Indigenous: the Manitoba Warriors, Deuce in Central, Indian Posse in the North End of Winnipeg. Those gangs were spreading through the prison-industrial complex across the country, into Regina, Saskatoon, Edmonton, Thunder Bay.

A special team of local and federal police, with armoured personnel carriers, full body armour, and fully automatic weapons, took down the house I had managed. They arrested all my uncles in the Manitoba Warriors. Everybody was arrested. Everybody went to jail and got put on the trial of the century. They even spent millions on a special court house. Eventually most of the cases fizzled and the anti-gang legislation they had created was ineffective. My uncle Brian had been the president for six or seven years, so he went down the hardest. The kid who took over for me got two years less a day. He went to Manitoba's Headingley Correctional Centre, one of the most notorious jails in the country. It was built in the early 1800s and the conditions were so bad, a prison riot broke out. One of the guards was captured in the riot, held hostage, and mutilated. That guy who took my place running the drug house I had quit operating was then sentenced to federal time in Stony Mountain Federal Penitentiary for his involvement in the riot. While he was in Stony Mountain, some incident went down and he was charged in another inmates death, and from what I hear, ended up getting even more time.

I never knew that kid's name. He was just another Native kid like me who had the dream job. But I always think: *That could've been me*. I could've been serving life in prison if my brother John hadn't sat me down that day and told me to do something more with my life, if Koren hadn't told me to get out. I'm so thankful to Creator that I was able to get away before I got in too deep. I'm grateful that my loved ones had the intuition to warn me, to shine a light on my positive attributes so I had the confidence to walk into the unknown.

nôtinikêwiyiniw

ᓅᑎᓂᑫᐃᐧᔨᓂᐤ

warrior

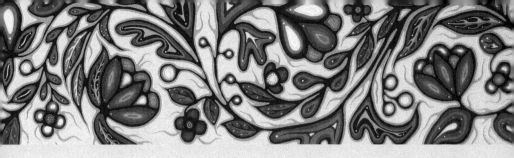

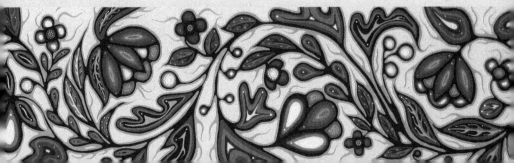

y uncle Alec is the most powerful man I've ever met. And he managed to save only half of the forest in our families trapline. I often wonder what it would have taken to save the whole thing.

Around the time I left the Warriors, Alec picked the fight of his life. Or I should say, the fight picked him. He had taken over occupancy of our family trapline. He was its guardian. So when a forestry-products company named Tolko showed up to clear-cut our trees, he knew it was his job to stop them.

They did get half the trees. Just took them. They left a wasteland of stumps and splintered limbs and charred slash-piles. My family was devastated. Something precious had been defiled. It was robbery, yes. But it was profanation. It was despoliation.

But Tolko picked the wrong dude to fuck with.

My first memory of Uncle Alec was riding to a funeral on his shoulders. There were a lot of funerals in Pukatawagan back then. He figures in another memory that helps explain why. In this memory, rifles are crackling outside our cabin. My mother roughly throws me under the bed, because bullets are punching through the wooden walls. She slides in beside me.

Then there is a ferocious pounding as the door is kicked in. My mother tells me to stay under the bed, no matter what I hear. She scrambles out, to where irons are heating on the woodstove. That's how she did the ironing back then. Irons were literally big wedges of iron. These ones are red hot, shimmering on the stove. When the door splinters open, she uses the iron as a weapon, sending the intruder to the floor.

"Fuck, Gail!" It was Alec, dodging bullets, now cradling a bloody burn on his face.

That was life in Pukatawagan back then. There was no gun control. Scores got settled in blood, and created new scores. Uncle Alec had been shot. He had been attacked with an axe. That was the way Alec lived. He was a badass.

If someone was clear-cutting his land, he was going to do something about it. But what could he do? He knew he was right. But Tolko had a permit. Alec wasn't a lawyer. He was a trapper. He had been raised in the bush. He spoke High Cree. He was not interested in pieces of paper signed by people he'd never seen, written in a language he didn't read, according to rules he had never been asked about. He just knew what was right.

So when the company train came up the tracks, carrying the men who would clear-cut the second half of the forest, he handled things with the tools he had: courage, and a rifle. He chained himself to the tracks. There he stood, in my mind, like that Chinese student in front of the tank in Tiananmen Square. Only he had a rifle.

And when he figured he needed more leverage in the negotiations, he brought it to his shoulder and fired a few rounds at the train.

The train backed up. It never came back.

Half of the forest in our trapline was saved. That's a victory. What about the other half of the forest, though? Our trapline is so far north that the trees there are small, stunted little jack pines. Tolko wasn't even making lumber out of it. They make something called OSB—oriented strand board, better known as chipboard. Woodchips and glue. They turned our forest into cheap sheeting for subdivisions. That was an irreplaceable loss.

And what about Uncle Alec? The train never came back, but the RCMP did, and Uncle Alec got two years in Stony Mountain for doing the right thing. That was what stayed with me. Being right wasn't enough. The rules turned the right thing into a crime. The rules legitimized the desecration of the forest and took away two years of my uncle's life.

I learned that justice isn't something you can count on. If you don't do anything to change the world, it is going to keep running along the same old tracks. If you want a different outcome, you need justice to roll along different tracks. I took inspiration from a half victory.

I also took inspiration from a half loss. The bravest, strongest man I knew wasn't quite strong enough. Alec was a warrior. He saved half a forest. I wanted to save the whole thing.

One of the mysteries of creation is how closely saving yourself and saving the world are linked. If you don't take care of the world, you will only end up harming yourself. And if you don't take care of yourself, you won't do the world any good. We're all part of the world. It is an illusion to think any of us can be separate.

I haven't figured these mysteries out yet, and I certainly hadn't figured them out when I was a skinny nineteen-year-old who had just left gang life, at least partly against my will. I knew there were big problems with the world, but even small problems were enough to keep me busy back then. I was broke. I had no high school education.

When you look at a maze from above, the way out is obvious. But when you're in the maze, all you can see is the wall in front of you. Turning back, or giving up, or pounding on the wall with your fists all look like options. Looking back, I can see that I had energy. I had ambition. But the challenge of the maze that kids like me face is not just the doing. It's the seeing. You have to see the way out.

It was my mom who showed me the crucial first step. If I hadn't taken it, my whole life would be different. It sounds crazy, but getting a résumé changed my life. She told me I wouldn't get anywhere without a résumé, and she was right. She may not have known how right she was.

Every Indian in Winnipeg knew that the place to go to get the most basic things done was the old train station. So with a shove in the right direction from my mother and with the words of my brother John ringing in my ears, I headed down to the Aboriginal Centre at Higgins and Main to get my shit together.

All I really wanted at the time was a couple of hours on a computer and a little advice so I could get a job. But I ended up signing up for a program called Anishinaabe Oway-Ishi. In Ojibwe that means "Native people leading the way." In Winnipeg there is an entire industry providing essential frontline social, employment, and education services to urban Indians, with a heavy focus on young people. Throughout the city, young people trying to get out of gang life or trying to claw their way out of poverty can apply to dozens of programs to learn basic skills, or search for a job, or access university or college. Anishinaabe Oway-Ishi was one of those programs.

You can talk all the theory you want, but if you want to see what is really going on with the Native community in a place like Winnipeg, check out a program like Anishinaabe Oway-Ishi. There are all kinds of ways to get your shit together, and I saw all the people trying to do it. Single moms in their forties. Young men and women, fresh off the rez, their first time in the city, wide-eyed and scared. Some were gang members trying to break out of that life before it was too late. I was a misfit who dressed entirely in black. I had dyed my hair completely pearl white and would often wear nail polish and makeup. This new look I was trying out was due to my emerging love of the underground warehouse scene which was pretty androgynous, queer, and gender fluid. Maybe I needed that program more than anyone.

It wasn't like I turned into an angel overnight. You don't go from dealing drugs and stealing cars to the straight-and-narrow path without any detours. At least I didn't. But the thing is, I found that program *exciting*. I hung out in the old train station all the time. I would rather have been there than out on the street. I guess that tells you something about why I did some of the things

I did. I'm not making excuses. I'm just saying that no one robs houses or looks for street fights when they're happy in life and confident that they're headed in the right direction.

I finished my high school diploma in that program, but I learned a lot more than math and history. One thing all those students had in common when we showed up was that we were all distrustful. There was a lot of swaggering and fuck-yous. Stupid jokes. Sullen silence. We were hard and fragile at the same time. Maybe the most important thing I learned, or began to learn, is that getting harder was not safer than opening up.

One thing we did every day was pull the chairs into a circle, burn some cedar or sweetgrass, and say a prayer. Then a small rock would be passed around the circle. When it came to your hands, it was your turn to open up. Maybe you would let the group know what was weighing on you. Maybe you would be worried about making rent. Maybe you were worried about your kid. Maybe you were worried your girlfriend was cheating on you. There are a lot of things that can gnaw at you when you're poor, and when you're finding your way out of the maze. Or maybe when the rock makes its way to you, you are moved to speak up and tell someone else in the group that you're there for them. That happened a lot.

But either way, it wasn't long before we started to see each other as complete human beings. Take care of the world, take care of yourself, right? The more we treated others with respect, the more we respected ourselves.

The thing is, if you get a bunch of Indians together in a room and they start to talk, eventually what you have is a political group. You can't be an Indian and not be political.

What I mean is, not being political is a luxury most Indians can't afford. That's for rich people, maybe. People without any problems. But if you are an Indian, and you have a problem of any kind, now you're in politics.

People think politics is about building support among stake-holders, or developing a message that changes public opinion and gets media attention, or holding power to account. It is all those things. But it's not only those things. Those things only matter when you have something to say. And what you have to say always comes down to what's fair. People will always demand what's fair.

That's why you can't be an Indian and not be political. Because at some point, you're going to know that things are not fair. I can't speak for my Black brothers, but I imagine it's the same for them. Just being Black probably makes you political.

I'm not saying that being Indian or Black makes you *right*. I've met my fair share of idiots, and they're not all the same colour. I've been an idiot myself, as you've seen. But when you know that your people have been treated unfairly, nothing is simple.

Was I turned down for that job because I'm an Indian, or was the other guy truly more qualified? Did the cops work me over because I'm an Indian, or is the cop just the kind of guy who would take any opportunity to bully someone vulnerable? You can't ever know the answer. But just asking the question is the first step into activism.

When I was hanging around the Aboriginal Centre, the questions we asked each other were always the same: Why are we so damn hard done by here in our own homeland? Why are we the poorest? Why are we in jail the most? Why do we have the highest rates of teen pregnancy? Or the highest rates of teen suicide?

These questions are not easy to answer. Not if you're being honest with yourself. But no one wants just answers. What we really want is justice. Understanding the way history intersects with the human heart can take a lifetime. But the fight for justice is something you can roll up your sleeves and wade into right away. And everybody in that program knew how to fight. We had been doing it our whole lives.

In fact, that whole building was crackling with a sense that something had to be done, and that we were the people to do it.

It's one thing to know that change is necessary. It's another thing to make change happen. Just about everyone wants to change things, but most of us never do. Why is that? It's not laziness, though it probably looks that way. But look closer. People are incredibly industrious. They're working their butts off. A lot of us are working just to provide ourselves and our families with the necessities. And that is a noble thing to work for. But if a new iPhone seems like a necessity to you, then maybe some of your energy is being channelled into pursuits that don't really benefit you, or the world. People say kids are lazy, but look at the hours they put into mastering something like *Fortnite* or skateboard tricks. They'll do the work if they think it's important, and if they're rewarded for it.

That's a long way of saying that if you want to change things, you need to be around people who want to change things.

I'd gotten to know a bro, Lawrence Angeconeb, who was always hanging around the Aboriginal Centre. Lawrence was older than me, and he was always talking about politics, treaty rights and the American Indian Movement, Dudley George, Leonard Peltier, and the Anicinabe Park occupation. He was obsessed with John Trudell, the poet from the American Indian Movement. Lawrence introduced me to the Medicine Fire Lodge program.

Medicine Fire Lodge was a federally funded program whose goal was to train Indigenous youth how to organize in our native community to develop and deliver social programming and gang intervention rooted in our culture.

Really, that's just a way to say that urban Indians need to find a way to fast-track the traditional immigrant process. Look at the Irish and Italian experience. When they showed up, they were treated like garbage. No one wanted them around. They were shunted into slums, where they excelled at the one opportunity left open to them: crime. They formed ethnic gangs, and those lucky enough to survive the brutal competition accumulated the resources to allow the next generation to become professionals or to invest in legitimate businesses. No one worries about the Irish mafia anymore.

So a group can go from poverty and crime to self-sufficiency pretty quickly. It happens. That's what we wanted.

Similarly to Anishinaabe Oway-Ishi, and just about every program at Higgins and Main, the participants in the Medicine Fire Lodge program were a hodgepodge of gangsters, single moms, young people who were trying to get somewhere in life. The program offered us a certificate in community development, but the administrators had so much more planned for us young people.

When people looking to change the world come together, they radicalize themselves. They push each other. Their dreams and their anger inspire each other. That's why it's important to be with the right people. And the people running Medicine Fire Lodge were men and women who had devoted their lives to their dreams and anger. A lot of them were old hard-core American Indian Movement–style Native activists who had ties to a lot of the revolutionary gang-intervention work in Watts in South-Central LA and to the Zapatista movement exploding in Chiapas at that time (1996–97). They had done a tremendous amount of work in Winnipeg and Native communities across Manitoba.

Since attending the 1990 UN Earth Summit in Rio de Janeiro, Larry and his brother, Vern Morrissette, had been busy networking with Indigenous academics, street gang leadership, and Indigenous business and political leadership. Leading up to Rio, Vern, a noted Indigenous academic here in Manitoba, worked with Indigenous leaders across the planet to produce a report called *Our Responsibility to the Seventh Generation*, which talked about the vital and crucial role of Indigenous Peoples' sacred connection to Mother Earth and how that knowledge, stewardship, and reference to the circle of life was the key to humanity's surviving capitalism and its symptoms, like climate change and war. The brothers took different approaches to this work, with the more extroverted Larry being embedded in the community, trying to address the gang pandemic that Winnipeg was facing in the 1990s.

Medicine Fire Lodge put a heavy focus on debate. They would bring in guest speakers who would talk about radical anti-racist theory, homophobia, misogyny, and break it down for us. We heard from guest speakers who were working to hold police accountable, sex workers talking about the fact that sex work is work and should not be criminalized, and Indigenous revolution-aries who had been involved in occupations such as Oka, Anicinabe Park, and Wounded Knee. We heard from guest speakers who were specialists in Indigenous sovereignty and human rights who unravelled systemic racism for us. We learned about Martin Luther King Jr., Malcolm X, and some of the lesser-known civil rights activists. We learned about our great Indigenous leaders, our great revolutionary leaders. We heard from leaders from all the differ-ent frontline community social service agencies about how they are barely getting by, just able to provide basic services. We learned also that colonialism is not just the historical crimes of those hungry for others' lands. It is also the mindset that drives the colonists. That same mindset will take over the thoughts of the colonized as well. If they're not vigilant.

Before the speakers came we would be assigned readings so that we'd be ready to engage with the topics they were speaking about. We would then have to debate each other, the guest pre-senter, and the program trainers about the topic. It was funny when we would get into the debates because many of my fellow Medicine Fire Lodge students had unfiltered and somewhat harsh perspectives that sometimes lacked empathy. When you put a bunch of current and former Indigenous gang members together and try to get them to have a high-level conversation, for example about the death penalty and its merits, you are going to see some wild shit.

I found this experience to be exhilarating, even though I almost got punched out a couple of times in the heat of debate. One of the participants was the nephew of Larry Morrissette, who never missed an opportunity to mention that he could kick my ass. He would also play devil's advocate and argue the perspectives of the white man. He wasn't the only one guilty of it— quite often the group's conversations would be sexist, homophobic, and generally harsh. For the entire duration of Medicine Fire Lodge, Larry's nephew threatened to kick my ass. He was massive. Thank god he didn't.

The other element of Medicine Fire Lodge that I found empowering was that often we would visit different ceremonial lodges and have Elders pray with us and light medicines like sage and cedar, tobacco and sweetgrass, and give us the teachings of these four elemental foundations in our shared Native culture. We would participate in community events and serve Elders at community feasts and celebrations. In this way I became close with many of the Native community leaders in the inner city of Winnipeg. My relationship with Larry Morrissette grew strong. He became a lifelong mentor. Larry taught me that there was no difference between Malcolm X and Martin Luther King Jr., that they were both complicated human beings who made many mistakes in their lives. But even though their paths were very different, they were both murdered by the white man.

Larry also taught me that the American Indian Movement was no different than the Manitoba Warriors in that both were community self-determination efforts aimed at healing our men, especially those re-entering the community after incarceration. And that many of the old AIMsters were old gangsters, drug dealers and pimps, just like all my older brothers in the Warriors. We always had to ask ourselves: Doesn't everybody have the right to heal?

Larry Morrissette was such a mystical being. If you were to meet him, he would come off as very unassuming. He had the vibe of some CIA operative, secretive, a man of few words. But he was a prophetic and poetic writer. He was a part of a vast global network of Indigenous activists that were all moving the goalposts of what was possible for Indigenous Peoples in their territories across the world. At the time I would romanticize how secretive he was and imagine I was being recruited to become an agent of the movement, in the way that the FBI would recruit someone into Quantico. It felt that intense.

And the fact is, once you're on that path towards justice, there is a momentum that keeps you going. It was around that time that I began to understand what the people around me meant by the word *warrior*. In fact, we regularly held induction ceremonies in which young Aboriginal Winnipeggers would officially become warriors.

AIM began as an idea not all that different from Black Lives Matter. Indians are no strangers to police brutality and the sort of racism that seeps into every aspect of everyday life, both in Canada and in the United States. Eventually, AIM started to focus on larger matters: treaty rights, sovereignty issues, environmental issues. AIM lawyered up.

But they were no strangers to direct action, or even to armed insurrection. The most notorious confrontation with the state came in 1973, at Wounded Knee. If you know what happened at Oka, it won't be hard to guess what happened at Wounded Knee. What began as a protest against poverty and treaty violation quickly escalated into an armed standoff that lasted seventy-one days. A federal marshal was shot and paralyzed, and two protesters were killed. Though the standoff ended shortly after that, the violence on the Pine Ridge reservation lasted for years, and as many as sixty more people died. FBI agents were killed, informants were executed. The fallout continues to this day. Leonard Peltier, one of the men involved in a shootout with the FBI, is still in prison for murder, despite pleas for clemency from Nelson Mandela, Mother Teresa, and the Dalai Lama and Amnesty International's challenge of his conviction. His next parole hearing is in 2024. So Wounded Knee is very much alive in the hearts of people who love justice.

I was inspired. Not by violence—I had seen enough violence that it had no romantic allure for me. In my mind, violence was something I associated with weakness rather than strength. Not that I condemned it on principle. Look at history. Sometimes justice needs a helping hand. But in my life, violence had all too often targeted the wrong people, the weak harming the weaker, or the strong lashing out in a moment of weakness. And to me, the warrior acts out of strength.

The person who uses violence to achieve a political goal is a soldier, not a warrior. A soldier may be brave, and may be honourable. But the fact is, in a best-case scenario, the soldier never has to resort to violence. Violence is just a tool.

But a warrior is defined by the struggle. Without struggle, he is something else. The struggle is in his heart. He can't put it aside on weekends, or retire from it. He is engaged with it. It holds him up, the way the air keeps a hawk in the sky. It is his purpose.

The curriculum Larry Morrissette and his team of facilitators exposed us young people to helped us connect the dots between poverty, colonization, and the colonial mindset that we were experiencing. It gave us the tools to be able, first, to organize our way out of our reality and, second, to have the strength and vision not to just get ourselves out of a tough situation but to rise up with our community. Most important, this Medicine Fire Lodge curriculum helped me begin the journey of living my life with dignity instead of pride.

It is not an easy distinction to keep in mind. To be honest, it has taken me years to hold on to this wisdom. But it became especially clear to me only years after I left Medicine Fire Lodge, when I was living in Vancouver. A friend of mine, Curtis Clearsky, was a Blackfoot guy who used to coach me. He was a mentor to me. He knew things that could help me, and he shared them.

He was a sober former member of the Native Youth Movement. I was battling to stay sober. I kept trying to blame other people. Curtis said to me: "It kinda sounds like you need to figure out how you are going to live your day, Clay. I hear you are upset with a lot of these people you mentioned. But when you wake up in the morning, you have to ask yourself, How am I going to live this day? Am I going to live this day worrying about what other people think about me or am I going to live this day thinking about how I feel about myself?" That really struck me. But that is not an easy journey.

When I was eighteen years old I started kicking it with young people from the Native Youth Movement who'd come out of Children of the Earth High School, or COTE, the first all-Native school in Canada, which is still there to this day. Children of the Earth was founded in the 1990s by a bunch of Native academics, including Priscilla Settee and Helen Settee, and many other leaders in the Native community. The curriculum was controlled by Indigenous Peoples to facilitate the decolonization of generations of young Native students, to free their minds from colonial thinking. Children of the Earth High School represented a turning point for Native control over our children's education in Canada. So many Indigenous Peoples had been affected by the legacy of attending residential schools and continue to carry the trauma that came with it.

For a high school to open up specifically for Native kids in Winnipeg, the biggest, most concentrated Native urban community in this country, was a sea-change moment. Finally we would have all-Indigenous school administrators, teachers, and support staff providing an Indigenous-created curriculum to Native kids. Almost every single member of the Native Youth Movement went to Children of the Earth High School. Some pretty revolutionary-minded students came out of COTE and went on to create the Native Youth Movement.

A lot of the young Natives at that time had witnessed horrific gang violence and were falling through the cracks: ending up in jail, in back alleys sniffing solvents, committing suicide. The 1990s in Winnipeg was a terrifying time. The federal and provincial governments' cutbacks to social programs impacted all poor communities and especially the Native community in our city. The direct consequences of cutting spending on education and the social safety net that Canadians take for granted meant that a lot of young Native kids that came into the city from the rez for education, or those who grew up here, ended up getting involved in gang activity just to make ends meet. The predatorial side of gang life and crime set up a situation where a lot of Native kids were getting recruited into street gangs. It even became a status symbol to be in a gang, to have your own money, to be able to afford nice clothes, to be able to leave money in your mom's mailbox for rent, to take your younger siblings to a movie at the Towne 8 Cinema, or go to the Red River Ex.

The Native Youth Movement was made up of young people who had all been touched by the gang epidemic of the 1990s, either being exploited directly or losing a loved one to murder or incarceration. A lot of these young folks came out of Children of the Earth High School and had been taught that all these circumstances could be turned around if we used ceremony and worked from a place of sacredness in partnership with our Elders.

The Native Youth Movement was started by the vision of Edee O'Meara, a Native activist in Winnipeg who had dreamed that the young people from the inner city would carry fire to both oceans. I often encountered Edee and other members at the Aboriginal Centre or at protests around the city. I often felt I was standing on the sidelines, but I took great inspiration from watching them speak powerfully in community about how we needed to change the fate of our people through changing ourselves.

A lot of the movement's political speeches and rhetoric—screamed through bullhorns out in front of the courts or the legislature—was rooted in teachings from ceremonial lodges woven together with experiences and stories from the American Indian Movement in the United States and the Red Power movement here in Canada.

One of the things that really inspired me and countless others was when these young leaders manifested Edee's vision and went out on the Sacred Walk. NYM members carried a fire from Winnipeg to Vancouver. It was people like Heather Milton-Lightning, Lawrence Angeconeb, Scott Benesiinaabandan, Tim Fontaine, my late cousin Harvey Sinclair, a lot of young people. They stopped in Native communities along the way, where they did workshops that spoke directly to the hearts and minds of young Native people with the goal of lighting a fire deep inside each individual heart so that these young people would also start doing the work in the community to stop our people from going to jail. Many people came to support them on that walk, gave them meals, paid for their hotel rooms and the gas for their support vehicles.

On that Sacred Walk, a horrific accident occurred in Alberta. A drunk driver hit the group. Edee O'Meara was seriously hurt, and her three-month-old passed away. Yet those young people kept walking, all the way to the Pacific Ocean. Years later they even walked to the Atlantic Ocean. I think they also went to the Gulf of Mexico. Edee and Heather and many of the other Native women in the Native Youth Movement reminded me so much of my mother, because even in the face of great, great adversity, they carried forward to make sure our people had what they needed to learn and grow and work past all the suffering and hurt we are collectively burdened by in the interest of achieving balance between our spirituality and the rest of our lives.

Inspired by the activism of all the members of the Native Youth Movement, several of us started a group called Aboriginal Youth with Initiative. The board and the staff were all Native youth. Staff was comprised of me, my buddies Lawrence Angeconeb and Heather Milton-Lightning, and the board comprised of some other young leaders from the community, such as Ken Sanderson. The idea was that young people could do the culturally appropriate community development work that young Indigenous Peoples needed.

Lawrence took a medicine wheel infographic from *The Mishomis Book*, by Eddie Benton-Banai, the lodge leader of the Three Fires Midewiwin Lodge. The infographic was a model for community self-determination that listed the clans, the clans' responsibilities, and which directions the clans were affiliated with. Lawrence applied that holistic governance model to our non-profit structure, so Aboriginal Youth with Initiative was modelled after a traditional clan system. Everyone had a line of accountability directly to the ED, and the ED had a line of accountability to the advisory committees and the board. It was a beautiful example of urban social programming based on a traditional Indigenous self-government structure. It was pretty groundbreaking for a non-profit. We also applied this model to our workshops, and it was how we talked about self-care and where change really begins. If you want to decolonize, start with the culture. That's what we did.

We would sit at Robin's Donuts all night long and drink coffee and smoke cigarettes until we got jittery. We'd talk politics all night and we'd be sober. We talked about changing everything, from education to welfare to healthcare. We talked about supporting programs in community policing to get our young people out of gangs and not just send them to prison.

Lawrence, Heather, and other members of the Native Youth Movement were very against incorporating under colonial systems but had a vision for growth that required a legitimate funding mechanism.

We started to realize that without being an incorporated registered charity, we were going to have a heck of a time paying for all the dreams we had. Organizing a powerful base of young revolutionary people that could hold our Native leadership accountable and challenge white people in power costs money. We weren't going to be satisfied with just talking.

Uncle Alec didn't just talk. Warriors don't just talk.

We needed to create a legitimate organization so we'd be eligible for grants to hire paid staff to support activists on the ground. Many Native Youth Movement members were studying for university degrees or had jobs and young children, or both. Full-time voluntarism wasn't sustainable. So we created Aboriginal Youth with Initiative to be able to hire paid organizers for our cause.

We managed to secure a $50,000 grant from my old mentor and friend Rick Magnus, at the Aboriginal Single Window initiative. And we created a partnership with the Aboriginal Council of Winnipeg to administer the funds we raised. We started going to work in all the inner-city high schools and community centres in Winnipeg, setting up workshops for the Native Youth Movement to run in collaboration with our staff to expand the reach and impact they already had through their volunteerism.

Now we could hire people to cook bannock and stew to feed people when they came to meetings. We could print out important information about the Native Youth Movement, about why we as Indigenous people needed to come together to combat police violence and the growing gang epidemic in the city, and about the need to tie that to the cultural revolution that had grown out of Children of the Earth High School. Instead of pipelines to prison, we were building a pipeline to Sundance.

The city was on board. We had unfettered access to school buses, community centres, gymnasiums, any kind of infrastructure that the city had that was not being used, we were able to use free of charge. This gave us, for the first time ever, an incredible ability to influence the chief of police, the mayor of Winnipeg, the premier of the province, and our own Indian political organizations.

Through Aboriginal Youth with Initiative, we were able to create the Assembly of Manitoba Chiefs Youth Council, which provided a voice in the decisions that Manitoba's over sixty First Nations were making that affected First Nations in the province. We were able to influence the Assembly of First Nations to create the First Nations National Youth Council and influence the decisions of the Assembly of First Nations and all First Nations across the country. And we participated in international events with Indigenous youth from across Mother Earth, through which we could reach into the United Nations with our ideas about revolutionary work grounded in our spirituality, culture, and language.

That's a lot of capital letters, I know. But put it this way. These were young people who had been dealing drugs only months or years earlier. Now we were taking that same hustle and appetite for risk and using it for good. I didn't have much education, but I had a PhD in hustle.

We would go into communities armed with our sacred pipes, medicine, and drums, not just to schools and organizations in the city but also to reserves all across Manitoba and Ontario. We would simply smoke our pipes and then talk about the need for decolonization, about what decolonization meant to us.

Most of us young Native leaders who were travelling around doing these workshops had been exposed to the original creation stories and the prophecies of the Ojibwe and Cree people. We share a prophecy that one day our children will be free from all the things that have been destroying our communities and have tormented our aunties, uncles, and parents before us. Many people believe that the generation I was a part of in the 1990s would be the one to find freedom, but that we would face risk. It was told down through the generations that we would hit a fork in the road. One path was the path of destruction and consumption and greed, it would be very difficult, and it would lead to the destruction of our people and our land and water. The other path was one of peace and abundance, one where our people could heal from hundreds of years of violence at the hands of the white man.

When we would talk to young people about reconciliation, we would talk about the prophecies. We would tie them into the work we were doing on reserves in terms of naming and directly intervening when we encountered injustice. When the prisons are full of young Native men and women, that's a call to battle. When our people are falling sick from environmental toxins, that's a call to battle. When despair seeps so deep into our hearts that our brothers and sisters contemplate suicide, that is an injustice that calls us to stand up.

A lot of us, because we had gone through Children of the Earth High School or another program in the Aboriginal Centre, knew very clearly that being reintroduced to ceremony and our language could counter the destructive behaviour in our community. A lot of our work was successful only when young people understood the importance of building a foundation for their human journey, a journey rooted in ceremony, in our traditional culture and language. That would lead to profound shifts in how we felt about ourselves and how people viewed us as we went out in the world to make a life. The more young people could get to ceremony and culture, the more powerful the force against the temptations that landed them in prison.

It wasn't perfect. Many of us were sober but a lot of us were not. There were always contradictions. Often people involved in the work and the movement would go through crisis. Many of them passed away, including my cousin Harvey Sinclair, who was one of the founders of the Native Youth Movement. Harvey got accused of some terrible things and started drinking again. He got tricked into drinking antifreeze that was in a vodka bottle. He was found in a back lane in Winnipeg. He was one of the most gifted artists that I had ever met. He used to babysit me as a little kid. Harvey's death was a tough lesson in how vulnerable we were and how important it was to stay on the right path and not fall back into old patterns. And if we did fall into old patterns, to be able to ask for help and ensure that we were not alone.

For me this work was Creator-blessed and Creator-led. That's the opposite of alone.

We offered everything from teen pregnancy-prevention programs rooted in our culture to decolonization workshops with high-risk kids attending inner-city high schools and after-school programs in Winnipeg community centres. Those programs led to a lot of direct gang-intervention work. We worked in the prisons, in juvenile detention facilities, in community spaces, and even out on reserves surrounding the city. We organized a couple of big national gatherings and brought in youth leaders from across the country who were fighting for sovereignty. All the while, we continued to do activism in the streets through the Native Youth Movement—much of our work organizing protests and vigils outside the Manitoba courthouse and at the provincial capital building.

It was not easy work. But as I said, Natives don't have the luxury of staying away from politics. You have what you believe in, or you have nothing at all. You say what you believe in, or else you're not telling the whole truth. Maybe saying what you believe in is easy, if what you believe in is easy. I wouldn't know. I do know that I was challenged at every turn. There is no shortage of opportunities to back down. But backing down won't get you anywhere.

Working in prisons is particularly difficult. Just the energy in a prison is intimidating, never mind the face-to-face interactions with people who are incarcerated. Especially in Stony Mountain, the federal penitentiary just outside Winnipeg that is one of the oldest penitentiaries in the country. Some of our greatest political leaders in history spent time there before their deaths: Louis Riel, the founder of Canada, and of course Chief Big Bear, one of the greatest chiefs to have ever lived. As idealistic young people immersed in lifting up the prophecies of our people, we certainly dealt with a lot of hostility and resentment from the young prisoners, especially gang members who were serving life sentences. The veterans in the prisons—those who had moved away from drug use and had been in prison pretty much their whole adult lives were now conducting ceremonies, running sobriety circles, and counselling young prisoners—would often intervene and open up the conversation in a way that we could share ideas and thoughts, rather than letting the conversations close down with a "Fuck you, I'm in prison for the rest of my life. Culture didn't do shit" explanation.

Aboriginal Youth with Initiative provided a platform of legitimacy for a lot of the young people who were answering the call of the Native Youth Movement. It gave us legitimacy to be able to access government, to comment on government initiatives and policies, and to make sure our communities understood what the federal government was doing with regard to young people. Within the first year, we were running a community centre full time and we were running programs in many community centres across the city. We grew from a small organization to one with a half-million-dollar budget and a dozen part-time staff operating in community centres, high schools, and after-school programs all across the city.

We were invited to various councils that the mayor of Winnipeg had put together to deal with the gang epidemic in the Native youth community. We were approached by Manitoba Health to do a program on teen pregnancy in all the inner-city high schools. We were able to create a number of advocacy vehicles, including the Assembly of Manitoba Chiefs Youth Council and the Assembly of First Nations National Youth Council. (I was the chair of both.)

Being on these youth councils gave the Native Youth Movement direct access to decision makers who were negotiating multi-billion-dollar transfer payments from the Canadian government to First Nations. Our point was that 75 percent of Indigenous people were under the age of thirty and 55 percent were under the age of twenty-five—and therefore young people needed to be involved in decision-making circles. For us, creating youth councils and facilitating organizing strategies that led to participatory democratic organization among young Native leaders through youth councils was a beautiful process of engagement. It had a snowball effect, generating some incredible buzz among decision makers, which led to a lot of opportunities for public and private funding to support our efforts in the community.

We were able to lobby the federal government to supply resources to inner cities for the disproportionate number of our young people who had become urbanized and were falling through the cracks, and who were in desperate need of programming. That led us to all kinds of international advocacy work: attending UN conferences and international forums all across Mother Earth, representing the collective rights of Indigenous Peoples from a youth perspective in all levels of jurisdiction. We were given $60,000 by the federal government, through Lloyd Axworthy in his role as Minister of International Affairs, to take a delegation to the 1998 International Indigenous Youth Conference in Waitangi, Aotearoa, also known as New Zealand, where the original treaty between the Maori and the British Crown was signed.

It got to the point where I was on a first-name basis with federal Attorney General Allan Rock, Ministers of Foreign Affairs Lloyd Axworthy and later Pierre Pettigrew, and Secretary of State for Children and Youth Ethel Blondin-Andrew. Many looked upon me as a poster child for effective social programming by Jean Chrétien's Liberal government. I participated, with Ethel and Pierre, in the Canadian delegation to the 1998 World Conference of Ministers Responsible for Youth, in Lisbon. Ethel took me to eat at the number one restaurant in Porto. The meal was to die for. The only thing I regret was that I was dead sober at the time. All that seafood without any wine!

Throughout those years I found myself elated—it was a big deal to be so young and leading an award-winning Native youth-led social movement organization. In six months, Aboriginal Youth with Initiative grew very quickly and we expanded from the founding three members of AYWI to a dozen, with four offices in inner-city community centres in Winnipeg. At nineteen years old, I was working as the executive director of Aboriginal Youth with Initiative and sitting on Winnipeg's gang-prevention committee alongside the mayor and the chief of police. Many of the skills I had acquired running a drug house for the Manitoba Warriors were completely transferable to working for the non-profit mafia in the inner city. For the first time in my life, I felt that I had gained the respect and recognition that I had yearned for.

Everyone from the mayor to Native leaders, to school administrators, to community centre leadership lifted me up as the poster boy for inner-city programs and how successful they can be in terms of impacting young impressionable Native youth. I was a high school dropout with a criminal record and had been involved with the city's gangs. I had benefited from many of the city's Indigenous programs for high-risk youth, from Anishinaabe Oway-Ishi to Medicine Fire Lodge to the Centre for Aboriginal Human Resource Development. I had won an Aboriginal Youth Achievement Award for co-founding Aboriginal Youth with Initiative because of my ability to adapt, assimilate, and talk the talk.

Through my role as the youth grand chief at the Assembly of First Nations, during Phil Fontaine's first administration, I was able to access funding at the administrative level. I was on a Heritage Canada committee that was designing funding distribution templates for a $350-million annual funding program called the

Urban Multipurpose Aboriginal Youth Centre Initiative. I gave a presentation to the committee that outlined how we would get young Native community leaders into elected positions in every single city in the country and how they would make the funding decisions for Native youth programming in every priority urban area. That approach ran for fifteen years, until Stephen Harper's Conservative government killed it. I always felt good knowing that, even for a time, I was able to influence a national process that put power back in the hands of capable young people.

When I left Aboriginal Youth with Initiative, my successor didn't work out so well. The organization didn't get its funding and shut down after about six months. But the Assembly of Manitoba Chiefs Youth Council and the Assembly of First Nations National Youth Council still exist. A lot of young leaders have come through those groups and gone on to do good things and helped their people in a good way. A lot of young people we worked with and who worked for Aboriginal Youth with Initiative went on to become great community leaders and have done amazing things.

I went to the University of Manitoba for one and a half semesters, but it was hard to leave activism—it was such rewarding and exciting work. I always found opportunities to work on reserves and offer decolonization workshops at youth conferences. Halfway through my second semester, I was offered a contract deep in the Amazon forest to train Indigenous leaders from North and South America on direct action, civil disobedience, decolonization, and cross-cultural alliance-building strategies. I weighed the options: winter in Winnipeg or Brazil? I dropped out of university.

While I was on this mission, I partook in the sacred medicine of the Yawanawá called uní. Many in the West know this medicine as ayahuasca. I was lying in a hammock deep in the jungle outside the northern city of Rio Branco. I had just finished puking my guts out, which is what happens before the medicine opens your mind and spirit. The forest talked to me and showed me the most brilliant vision. I remember my spirit flying across the jungle like an eagle and seeing the most vivid greens. That night I saw the spirit of the rainforest and it became a part of me forever. I will never forget the songs of the Elder who guided us that night.

Real education isn't about learning facts. It's about seeing patterns. From a certain perspective, my uncle Alec's act of armed defiance is an outlier. It was front-page news. But from a wider perspective, it was all too familiar. It's the way the world works. People with money and power try to push Indigenous people off their land. Sometimes they get away with it. In fact, they've got away with it most of the time over the centuries. But sometimes the rightful stewards of the land push back. It might be a single badass, like Uncle Alec. Or it might be a whole bunch of badasses, like the Zapatistas.

I marvel now that it took me so long to see the similarities between what was going on in my uncle Alec's trapline and the injustices in Chiapas, Mexico. Back in the 1980s, parts of Mexico were farmed the way they had been since the revolution—that is, small communities, many of them Indigenous Mayas, farmed the land they shared, as they had for generations. But small-scale subsistence farming is not very interesting to international capital investment, which is what the Mexican government was looking for. So the government just privatized the land.

But you can't sell what you don't possess—just as lumber companies can't cut down trees they can't get to. The difference between Jetait and Chiapas, however, is that Uncle Alec acted on his own. In Mexico, the Maya farmers acted together. The Zapatista movement (named after an agrarian reformer in the revolution) had been around for almost a decade by that time, protecting farmers from eviction and bullying, but when eviction became a matter of government policy, there was no way back from open confrontation with the police and even the army.

Hundreds have died in the struggle. Though the conflict is far from over, the Maya are still farming their land today. That is a victory in itself.

But the cost of resistance can be shocking. In 1997, a right-wing paramilitary group burst into a small church in the Chiapas village of Acteal. They slaughtered the people inside, killing forty-five, including pregnant women. The worshippers belonged to a group of non-violent Indigenous activists who called them-selves The Bees (*Las Abejas*). But as often happens, the killers only inspired the resistance. As reports of the carnage spread around the world, activists quickly realized what before might have seemed more like rhetoric than a concrete truth: we were in this together. In a show of solidarity, Indigenous activists from around the world converged on Chiapas.

I was one of them. I was nineteen.

The idea for the exchange was built on the collaborative work that had been done by Indigenous Peoples from Manitoba, the state of Oaxaca, and one of the states in northeastern India who had worked on a report called *Our Responsibility to the Seventh Generation* that had been produced by Larry and Vern Morrissette for the first Earth Summit, in Rio de Janeiro.

That report was the basis of the curriculum that I followed as a young organizer, when I got my first training through the Medicine Fire Lodge program, which Larry had created. It is in fact the foundation of my entire career. Its anti-colonial lan-guage and anti-capitalist analysis are still relevant today. Through that report, I was introduced to Indigenous people speaking for themselves about extractivism and about how multinational corporations and bilateral free-trade agreements and neoliberal economic theory were fundamentally at odds with, and disproportionately disrupting, Indigenous Peoples' economies around the planet. The report argued that Indigenous restorative value-based economies and trade were the key to addressing the issues of the day.

What I saw in Oaxaca shocked and troubled me. I had learned the theory of colonialism. I knew the facts. I even knew the experience. Facts are one thing. Seeing the poverty and violence of my brothers' and sisters' lives was a slap in the face. To this day, their jobs on the coffee and fruit plantations are little more than indentured slave labour. Families live in shacks owned by the plantation barons. And they live there only during the eight months there is agricultural work to do. For the other four months, the doors are locked. Parents leave their children at the Catholic-run orphanage to travel to the free-trade zones up north in Juárez, south of Brownsville, Texas, where all the television and car factories are. That's where all the free-trade manufacturing happens. Why do companies relocate to Mexico? Dirt-cheap wages. Mexican auto workers earn even less than their Chinese counterparts. But even that is a lot more than they make in Oaxaca. So a lot of kids' parents don't come back. A lot of the women, the mothers, don't come back. They have a murdered and missing Indigenous women problem in Mexico just like in Canada, but way worse. Tens of thousands of women disappear in Juárez.

In Oaxaca, Larry took my friend Lawrence Angeconeb and me to a storming of the presidential palace. We drove down the mountain into the city in a Volkswagen Beetle, and I had terrible motion sickness from all the winding roads. There were many different political movements at the rally. The various militants were separated by colourful ropes so that each political group had their own section of courtyard. The palace was an impressive building, with cobblestone courts and a Spanish Colonial facade. To participate in overwhelming it with Indigenous revolutionaries defied my perception of the world. Many of the Zapatistas who had marched to Mexico City in protest of the military's massacre of teachers in Chiapas were barefoot. Imagine walking from Vancouver to Fort McMurray barefoot.

As we were rolling into the rally, Larry said, "People might think you're gringos. Gringos down here are anybody from the north. But just show 'em your status card and you should be all right. Just make sure they know you're Indigenous."

I remember thinking: *What the hell! These fuckers have guns.* At that moment, this really powerful man who looked like he was the boss of everything—he had white hair, white pants, a white button-up short-sleeved shirt, and a red bandana around his neck—walked up to Larry and hugged him.

Larry said, "Hey Gustavo, how's it going, bro?"

Gustavo said, "Larry, my friend! It's nice to see you. Who are these people?"

Larry told him, "These are young Indigenous men from where I come from. I wanted them to be here and experience this."

Gustavo embraced us and introduced us to some of the warriors. Here began the armed uprising in Chiapas. The Zapatistas, peasant farmers, were marching to Mexico City to protest the unjust treatment of them and their Indigenous rights, and to defend the sovereignty and self-determination of their land and resources. We stayed there all night. One of the Zapatistas gave me his mask. I had never gone to a big protest like that before. Being in a foreign country, and rolling into this big political demonstration with this old gangster from the inner city of Winnipeg, and seeing such huge numbers of Brown people take a government seat, was amazing. I wanted to grow up and be like Larry. I remember explicitly thinking, *I want more. I want to know more about this.*

Activism is not easy to define. You do it for yourself, and you do it for others. Sometimes it requires you to follow the rules, and sometimes the right path is to break the rules. Sometimes you appeal to others' sense of what is right, and sometimes you know that will be a waste of time. Sometimes it means collaboration and compromise, and sometimes it is raw confrontation. Sometimes you ask for what is fair, and sometimes you have no choice but to just take it.

In that moment, caught up in a life-and-death struggle, I had a new understanding of my uncle's courage and despair, and a sharpened sense of what it means to be a warrior. It means losing yourself a little in the energy of the people you're fighting along-side, and also finding yourself in that part of your spirit you know will never back down.

One thing I learned in Mexico is that nothing is local. Wherever there are Indigenous people, there are sovereignty fights. There are murdered and missing women. There is violence and sub-stance abuse. And there are warriors holding their heads high. I wanted to meet and work with these warriors. So I went to California. I was young and impulsive. I was looking for action.

Things didn't go quite as I had planned there. I didn't have a job. I was broke. I had learned a lot, but ultimately California seemed to defeat me. Moving back to Canada appeared to be the only option. I was literally packing my bags when I got a phone call from Tom Goldtooth, the executive director of the Indigenous Environmental Network, or IEN. He had heard me on a panel where I had spoken emotionally about the link between environ-mental injustice and downstream consequences for Native com-munities. He said, "Those were some good words you said. Do you want to go for lunch?" I said, "OK, sure. I got nothing to do." So he told me, "Meet me at Project Underground in Berkeley."

Project Underground was a cutting-edge NGO that sup-ported communities affected by mining and oil and gas compa-nies all across the planet. When I showed up in the boardroom, Tom was accompanied by the entire board of Project Under-ground, including the executive director. It ended up being an interview for the position of IEN's North American Indigenous climate and energy campaign director.

Tom laid it out. "IEN has a partnership with Project Underground called the Indigenous Mining Campaign Project. We're going to expand that project to include an oil campaigner position because in Indian Country, we've got so much pressure coming from oil and gas companies, coal companies, fossil fuel companies that we need somebody out there on the ground organizing in these communities across Turtle Island. Do you want the job?"

Sayo':kla Kindness, an Oneida activist and board member, said, "Hold on, Tom. We haven't even talked to Clay yet. You need to let us ask questions."

Tom said, "Oh. OK. Sorry. Go ahead."

The board started asking me questions about my work in Manitoba with young people and lobbying the federal government. They asked me, "Do you feel comfortable travelling and taking on some of the biggest corporations on the planet and organizing in different communities under extreme circumstances? Can you take orders and execute political objectives without any fear?"

I said, "Hell, yeah! No problem. I've been doing that my whole life."

Of course my life wasn't all that long at that point, but I was offered the job. I needed it. I was so broke, I would have worked at California's beloved In-N-Out Burger. But it was more than a job. Much more. Having the attention of Tom Goldtooth in the absence of any father figure was so flattering, even if I didn't quite know what I was getting myself into. It washed away any doubts I may have had. When I became Tom's right-hand man, I suddenly had purpose.

When I started working with IEN, one of the United States' oldest and most respected environmental justice organizations, Tom Goldtooth instructed me, "You've got to learn how to work with our Native people. You've got to learn about the history of the environmental justice movement." He taught me the seven principles of a Native organizer, a model he had developed based on the seventeen principles of environmental justice but tailored to our Native worldview and cosmology.

Tom is a genius. He is touched by Spirit. He said to me, "There's all these little fires burning—in Oklahoma, in the Great

Plains, in Alberta, in Alaska, the Gulf Coast, California, up in the Northeast, Penobscot territory. I need you to go there and unite those little fires into one big fire."

Then he sent me out into the world.

Tom told me the story of how IEN started. The group grew out of a fight in the early 1990s. The US Department of the Interior was working with incineration companies and it wanted to place waste incinerators in Indian Country. They called it economic development. Some of those incinerators were slated for the Navajo Nation. The Elders there were not interested in that kind of development. They were already living with Peabody Energy, a coal-mining company. They were already seeing their water poisoned and their land destroyed.

For fifty years, Peabody Energy had been allowed to run amok on Navajo lands and destroy the lives of the Diné people, removing them from their hogans and relocating them to get at the coal underneath their sheep-grazing lands. So the Elders asked the young people to do something about this new form of "development," which they feared was little more than an attempt to dump toxic waste on Native lands. The result was the first Protecting Mother Earth conference, in Dilkon, Arizona. Tom, who is a Diné Dakota from around Crownpoint, Navajo Nation, was one of those young people, and in the years since, he has become a respected activist and a leader in the environmental and economic justice movement.

Tom told me, "You are going to start your journey in Navajo. I want you to travel the whole nation and I want you to audit all of the transmission lines, all the pipelines, all the oil and gas extraction, all the coal mines, all the energy infrastructure in the Navajo Nation." The Navajo Nation is as big as some countries in Europe. It is the biggest Indian reservation in America, covering four states, Colorado, Utah, New Mexico, and Arizona, that come together in a place within the Navajo Nation called Four

Corners. Tom instructed me to connect with Diné CARE, one of IEN's founding organizations that had been fighting for the protection of Big Mountain and fighting against the relocation of Diné and Hopi people by Peabody Energy. This is a decades-old fight lead by grassroots Diné Peoples against coal mining in their sacred lands.

Tom said, "I want you to hang out with the young Diné people. They're starting an organization. I want you to help them, and to travel across their nation, with Wahleah Johns and Enei Begaye." Wahleah and Enei were founders of Black Mesa Water Coalition, a youth organization set up by Diné youth to stop coal strip mining in the Black Mesa region of Navajo Nation. I travelled across that nation and I saw things I'd never dreamed of. Seeing all these places on this journey, I got a real sense of just how dependent on and wrapped up with extractivism our Native nations are, how they had been given shitty deals by the trust relationship with the US government.

Uranium mining and coal mining and other extractions have been taking place in Navajo Nation for over a century, much to the detriment of the local Navajo and Hopi people. There's a long history of forced relocations in the Navajo Nation, and there's a long history in the Navajo Nation of resistance to Peabody Energy and multiple uranium-mining companies. Although many of those companies aren't operating now that there's a moratorium in place, they left a damaging legacy because they sent Navajo miners into the mines without any kind of protection, without any ventilation, without any air or water. Miners would drink groundwater leaking from the uranium walls. They would go home with uranium dust on their clothes. Their wives would be exposed to the uranium and their children would be exposed when their wives would do the laundry. A lot of people died—and continue to die—from cancer.

I spent three weeks there and I drove five thousand kilometres, looking at all the pipelines, all the transmission lines, all the coal-mining operations, all the uranium mines that had been decommissioned but never cleaned up. I talked to people about how they felt about these industries being in their homeland and the effect it had on their way of life and on their human rights. It was a big eye-opener for me, especially given that the Southwest is one of the most beautiful places on Earth. It's like you're on Mars, but you can breathe and the people are really nice.

Something clicked in me there. Something I'd somehow learned from Uncle Alec but had not fully registered: There is no justice without environmental justice. The plundering of the land is the plundering of the people. When the land is polluted, the people are polluted.

After I returned from Navajo Nation, I went to the state of Oklahoma, where I learned how a hundred years of oil and gas operations had devastated the state. I learned that America had forced over a hundred thousand Native Americans to relocate during what was called the Trail of Tears. Oklahoma, where the Trail of Tears ended, has thirty-six tribal nations, although only five or six are actually from Oklahoma. The rest were sent there from northeastern or southeastern states and from around the Great Lakes and the Dakota regions. Whatever land the colonists wanted, they first cleansed of its Indigenous people. The refugees were sent to Oklahoma, on foot. Thousands died along the way. But Oklahoma was the designated state for Native Americans. It was supposed to be a little country within a country. But when the colonists discovered oil in Oklahoma, they took that away from them too.

I spent a lot of time in Oklahoma mentoring under Jan Stevens, who came from Sac and Fox Nation. The Sac and Fox people had originally come from the Great Lakes but had been displaced to Oklahoma like so many others. Jan's father, an amazing Elder who has gone on to the spirit world, told me about his tribe's struggle to find food and to build their ceremonial cattail lodges in Oklahoma. He took me to his cattail lodge, which looked like a sweat lodge but was made out of cattails, just like back up north.

Jan was a tribal Environmental Protection Agency scientist. She worked for her tribe and ran their environmental protection office. Jan mentored Tom Goldtooth. Tom told me, "If you're going to work on energy, I need you to know the science." Tom's mother was an astute believer in science, a Diné woman who acquired two degrees in the United States during a time when it was very hard to do so. Tom took science very seriously. He said to me, "You've got to be able to break down thermal power plant engineering. You've got to be able to break down all the technology of coal-bed methane. You've got to know the engineering of all of this stuff so that when you debate these industry types, you can go toe to toe with them. You've got to learn the policy. You've got to learn about the Environmental Protection Act. You've got to learn about the National Historic Preservation Act. You've got to learn about the Department of the Interior, the Bureau of Indian Affairs, the Department of Energy. You've got to learn the bureaucracy."

Tom sent me to stay with Jan for a couple weeks and learn from her. She was the board member of IEN that I was most scared of. She was a very traditional Native woman and very strict. Her braid was to her knees. She expected a certain level of respect. She had that southern Oklahoma thing going on: you called her ma'am. Jan knew the EPA and environmental regulations and enforcement mechanisms in the United States inside out. She knew all about the century-old legacy of oil and gas development in Oklahoma.

Because the only way for land-ownership transfer to happen in that state is through inheritance, there's a long, sordid history of white American men who took Native American wives who then came to untimely deaths. Thus the white men could get to the oil under the land that was now theirs. Some men had eight different Native wives who had died. Since these men inherited their wives' government-designated parcels of land, they became modern-day barons, ruling over vast tracts of land that had been part of Indian reservations not even a generation earlier. That's why in Oklahoma to this day, there are a lot of checkerboard Indian reservations, with Native land interspersed with white land.

I had always been angry. But Oklahoma kindled something different in me. A new fury smouldered in me.

Jan drove me around the state and showed me the oil well heads that had never been sealed and were leaking radioactivity. (Yes, radioactivity. Oil extraction draws all kinds of heavy metals up to the surface.) She showed me the corroded pipelines, the tank farms built on burial sites. She showed me the Ponca City ConocoPhillips refinery, which is right across from the Ponca Nation cemetery. The American Indian Movement activist Dwain Camp, who is a veteran of the 1970s Wounded Knee occupation, lived right by the ConocoPhillips refinery. He dug a two-foot hole in his front yard, pulled up a can of groundwater, and poured it into his lawnmower. Then he put the cap on and fired up the mower. The hydrocarbons in his groundwater were concentrated enough to power the motor. That's how contaminated their land is.

We did a lot of work advocating for the remediation of old abandoned oil infrastructure in Oklahoma with Jan and with the Sac and Fox Nation. But after Jan was killed in a car accident by a drunk driver, that work stalled for a while, until my auntie Casey from Ponca picked it up. Auntie Casey is another powerful grandma. She has been one of the main voices in the Keystone XL campaign and also at Standing Rock. She was at Wounded Knee. She is a star. She was in the movie *Lakota Woman* and many other films. Carter Camp, Casey's big brother, was the last AIM member to leave Wounded Knee. Carter told me the story about how he caught an FBI agent who had snuck into Wounded

Knee and he beat his ass and pocketed his chrome-plated .45. He took that guy over to the front line in Wounded Knee, all beat up, and he tossed his ass over to the other FBI agents and said, "Here. One of your guys got lost."

Navajo Nation has become the battery powering cities, including Phoenix, Louisiana, and Las Vegas. All the coal-fired power plants that provide energy to these cities—so that people living in a desert can have air conditioning twenty-four hours a day and can water their golf courses—come at a huge cost to the Navajo Nation. The coal is mined, ground into dust, then mixed with water and piped four hundred kilometres to the Mohave Generating Station. That requires approximately sixty-two billion litres of water. Where does that water come from? It is pumped out of the desert. It is polluted. It is stolen. Much of my work at that time was collaborating with Navajo non-profits to try and put a stop to this theft of water in their dry arid desert land.

I also took on a bunch of other files. In Montana and Wyoming I helped to fight the coal-bed methane boom, and in Medicine Lake, in northern California, I helped the Karuk, Yurok, Shasta, Hupa, Yana, Pit River, Wiyot, and Wintu tribes in their fight to stop a company from building a geothermal energy plant on a sacred hot spring that the tribes had used as a healing place for thousands of years. I worked with dozens of other communities as well.

I travelled to all these places to support local grassroots activists in their campaigns to stop fossil fuel companies from encroaching on their lands. This included campaign skill-shares like how to map out your allies and your enemies, how to mobilize community, how to do slick media campaigns, how to use narrative-based storytelling strategies (although that wasn't what we were calling it at the time), and how to use the moral authority that we had as community people negatively affected by multinationals and their operations.

Over the years I really loved it when the companies we were organizing against debated us in the media or at community consultations or shareholder meetings; they would always come across as big evil capitalist corporations whose only bottom line is profit, not human rights. The one thing they can't say is the truth. Every time we would engage them in the media, they would express frustration with Indigenous rights being a barrier to their profits, which was pretty damming to their social capital and brand.

Through my position with the Indigenous Environmental Network, I got to work with Sarah James, a respected Gwich'in Elder from Arctic Village, Alaska, and meet my good friends Faith Gemmill and Evon Peter, also from Arctic Village, all of whom were leading the fight to protect the Arctic National Wildlife Refuge, up in the North Slope of Alaska, from oil drilling. Alaska is the fourth most polluted state in the country because of toxic pollution sites. Oil companies have been allowed to run amok. I went to Alaska to help them start the statewide organization called REDOIL—Resisting Environmental Destruction on Indigenous Lands—a coalition of seventeen Alaskan Native nations that has been taking on mining companies and big oil companies in the state since 2007.

Every year we would hold a feast at the Hilton Anchorage during the Alaska Forum on the Environment, a greenwashing conference organized and sponsored by Big Oil, the state EPA, and the US military. Every year the forum would fly all these Alaska Natives to the conference. Industry would be there, and senators and oil people would speak and get their pictures taken with real live Inuit.

REDOIL called their "green" bluff. We held a feast and panel event called "Stories from the Struggle." We would lift up the voices of Alaska Natives who would talk about their fight against the military-industrial complex and against Big Oil, companies like BP, ExxonMobil, Shell. Natives would bring country food from all across the state—it was how we got the Natives to come to our event. I had it worked out with the Hilton so that even though staff were unionized, we could serve country food; in our contract we called it a "taste-testing." We had cari-bou from three different North Slope herds, salmon from eight different rivers in Alaska including the Copper, herring eggs, polar bear, three different types of whale, walrus—they were crazy feasts. Our event got so big that there would be nobody at the hundred-thousand-dollar banquet at the Alaska Forum on the Environment. Everyone, including the industry, govern-ment, and military bigwigs, would be at our feast.

In 2005 Senator Ted Stevens was at the forum. Stevens was one of the guys who in 1971 had ushered in the Alaska Native Claims Settlement Act, which stripped Alaska Native tribes of their tribal membership and turned the tribal governments into thirteen Alaska Native corporations. Native tribal members became shareholders in those corporations. The sole purpose of the Alaska Native corporations is to generate revenues through mega-extraction projects. It was a federal act, an experiment in the Indian termination policy of the US government. In this way, Senator Stevens poisoned the Alaska Inuit communities.

It's the oldest trick in the book. Colonists always set up a privileged caste drawn from the native population to administer their interests. The Greeks and Romans did it; the Ottomans and British did it. Give a small group of locals a piece of the action, and they'll do your dirty work. In fact, they become addicted to your dirty work. So in many instances these Native corporations end up being just as bad as the oil companies. They're working hand in hand with Exxon, with BP. The Fort McKay Cree Nation in the Alberta tar sands is corrupted by the same invest-ment in extraction. They're profiting from their own demise.

That year, Senator Stevens was speaking at BP's conference, in a room that holds a thousand people or more, but the room was empty except for two people. Everyone else was at REDOIL's counter-event, feasting on country food and learning about strategies to stop the spread of Big Oil. It was deeply satisfying to be able to stick it to Senator Stevens like that.

In Canada today, and to a lesser degree in the United States, people are comfortable calling out mainstream, corporate media when it imposes non-Indigenous labels on Indigenous people— it's called extractive storytelling, and it's a form of institutional racism. Don't call me a "protester" when I call myself a "water protector"; don't call me an "eco-terrorist" when I call myself a "land defender." The corporate media is not entitled to choose a name for me.

Native pride is such that people are comfortable defending their sacred spaces, especially when they're being documented. But the discourse around decolonization and white supremacy and patriarchy is different around the world. In 2002, I was part of the IEN delegation to the World Summit on Sustainable Development, in Johannesburg, and we were hosted by the Khoisan people. They're sometimes known as the world's first people, as they were the first inhabitants of southern Africa. You might know of the Khoisan people from the film *The Gods Must Be Crazy*. They have faced wave after wave of colonialism, of African tribal colonialism and then European.

We had negotiated terms with the Khoisan people to organize an Indigenous pre-summit on sustainable development in Kimberley, South Africa, home of the infamous De Beers diamond-mining corporation. This company enslaved South African Black people in the notorious mine in Kimberley. It's a huge hole in the middle of the city that goes one and a half kilometres down. We held our conference right beside that hole and talked about colonialism within the context of sustainable development.

Many young Indigenous leaders—from big fights like Black Mesa and the fight to protect Navajo lands from coal mining, to representatives from Alaska and the Yukon fighting against drilling in the Arctic National Wildlife Refuge—attended the World Summit on Sustainable Development as part of our delegation. I had just gotten married in Oakland a month before, and so my wife came with me to South Africa. Koren says that was no fucking honeymoon but it was definitely an experience.

As part of the World Summit, nicknamed Rio+10, our Khoisan hosts performed an ancient ceremony to honour the full moon. They were doing a dance in the middle of the desert outside Johannesburg and they were naked. We were all in a circle, there was a fire, there was a full moon. It was very sacred. All the media people were up in their faces. One guy, an Afrikaner with what seemed like a floodlight on his rig, went right up in the middle of a circle and was recording up their behinds. I was shocked, but nobody was saying anything. I lost my temper. I was a little more fiery back then. I walked right into the circle of a thousand people. I grabbed that guy by the scruff of his neck and I dragged him out of the circle and yelled, "Get some goddamn respect! They are doing a sacred ceremony. Don't be filming up on them! See any of us going in filming during the sacred ceremony? Turn the goddamn light off on your camera!"

He realized that I was a foreign national and was not going to back down and he said, "Fine, then."

When the ceremony ended, my Khoisan friends came up to me and asked, "What was that all about?"

I said, "Why didn't you call him out?"

They told me, "They always film us like that." They were amazed that I had manhandled the guy.

Later I realized that I was projecting my Western-centric experience with settler colonialism in a place where there is hyper-militarization. Black folks in South Africa were still getting disappeared all the time, among them Indigenous Black folks like the Khoisan, who are an incredibly marginalized group. I should've gone up to my Khoisan brother and said, "I'm going to go up and grab this jerk. Is that OK?" I should have gotten that consent. You can never project your experience on anybody else. It trips you up. I do it to this day. I get agitated with what I see happening in the movement, but everybody is a product of their own environment and everybody's reality is real to them.

At that time I began to organize a lot of delegations to Washington, DC—or as we call it, Washington Deceit —to lobby Congress on Indian energy policy. President George H. W. Bush and Dick Cheney, those leaders of the free world, were trying to pass an energy bill that included Title V, legislation that would kick open the back door to Indian Country to big fossil fuel interests. Title V was designed to give American Indian nations the right to approve and regulate their own energy projects. Of course it was a setup, because there are only a couple of tribes with the legal and scientific capacity (including their own environmental protection departments) to actually preside over big energy projects. This legislation would essentially result in energy projects being built without any federal oversight, because the tribes don't have any oversight capacity and the government wasn't giving any money to them to provide oversight. The bill would have continued to build upon the legacy of subsidizing and giving corporate welfare to the richest, most powerful corporate entities that ever graced the Earth.

I created alliances with grassroots groups in Alaska Native nations and with a lot of people in about thirty nations in the Lower 48. We began to go to Washington to talk to congressional leaders. Through direct actions, lobby trips, and slick media campaigns, we were able to defeat that first energy bill. It was a big victory, and it was the direct result of our people working together and lobbying not only congressional leaders but also our own leaders.

We got the National Congress of American Indians—the US equivalent of the Assembly of First Nations—and many other institutions to target our champions in Congress, leaders like Senator Daniel Akaka from Hawaii. Akaka, at the request of the National Congress of American Indians and all the tribal nations that we were working with through our campaign, killed the energy bill in the Senate. It was one of the biggest victories in my young professional career. I got to smack out President Bush and Dick Cheney in their own yard. Of course, when their second term came around, they slammed that energy bill right through. But that's the ebb and flow of things—in this work as a campaigner, it is always a "one step forward, two steps back" scenario. But every victory in the Indigenous rights and climate justice movement leads to thousands more joining our ranks as we build the largest social movement ever in the history of our people.

During Bush and Cheney's second administration, there was a massive push to open up the Arctic National Wildlife Refuge in the North Slope of Alaska and to expand energy development in Indian Country right across the board. My job became increasingly tense because it was often me who would be in direct contact with community members, and I was working with many communities. Our organization wasn't leading the campaigns— we were supporting those who were leading the campaigns. But the campaigns became very real life-and-death situations.

In Alaska, the Arctic National Wildlife Refuge is the end of the line. It's on the Arctic Coastal Plain, right on the Arctic Ocean on the other side of the massive Brooks mountain range. The Gwich'in people live in that mountain range. They are Athabaskan Dene and they're the most northerly Native Americans in continental North America. This is the last remaining Indigenous nation to subsist off a wild herd of animals. Like the Prairie Natives who subsisted on the buffalo until the nineteenth century, these people continue to subsist off the Porcupine caribou herd, which migrates each fall from their calving grounds on the North Slope all the way into Yukon for the winter. Twelve Gwich'in villages are along that migration path, and so every time the caribou come through, they get what they need for their food, their clothing, their cultural needs.

All twelve Gwich'in villages know that you don't mess with the caribou when they're giving birth to their babies. Of course the US Congress and Big Oil don't know this. They wanted to drill for oil there, although at the current rate of US consumption, there was only six months' worth of oil in the Arctic National Wildlife Refuge. Did they really want to go to all that trouble for only six months' worth of oil? We know now that they were just trying to build the infrastructure for offshore oil and gas development, which Shell is aggressively trying to develop on the outer continental shelf. Through our organizing work in Alaska, I was able to help Alaskan Native leaders create the REDOIL Network.

Working up in Alaska was a very powerful experience. Alaskan Natives face a similar situation to the First Nations in northern Alberta in the midst of the tar sands. Big Oil is present in every institution, whether it's education or the arts. Every building in downtown Anchorage bears a logo of a Big Oil company. When I looked out over Cook Inlet from my hotel, you could see thirteen oil and gas offshore platforms. You can see their flares rising sixty metres into the night sky. All of them are exempt from reporting how much toxic effluent they pour into the inlet every year.

We beat the Bush-Cheney beast again in their second term and the oil companies did not drill in the Arctic National Wildlife Refuge. That said, that administration doubled down and opened up the National Petroleum Reserve to oil and gas leasing. The NPR is a vast region in northwestern Alaska that is just as biodiverse, as rich, and as fragile as the Arctic National Wildlife Refuge.

With every sacred place that is saved, two, three, four, five sacred places are opened up to mega-development. One step forward, two steps back.

For the first year of my work with the Indigenous Environmental Network, I was mentored by Project Underground, which had partnered with IEN on what was called the Indigenous Mining Campaign Project. For a couple of years, my IEN colleague Sayo':kla Kindness had been fighting the mining sector and their encroachment into Indian Country. Just like energy companies, the mining companies were disproportionately targeting our communities with their promises of a quick fix to our economic woes: all we had to do was change the way we related to the sacredness of Mother Earth and embrace the industrialization game. We all know this is just a form of neo-colonization.

At that time, Project Underground was one of the most radical human rights organizations on the planet fighting against the mining and energy sector. It was supporting frontline Indigenous leaders in such jurisdictions as Ecuador, West Africa, Nigeria, Southeast Asia, and Indonesia in their fight to protect their lands and waters from Big Oil and mining. I was mentored under Project Underground's board chair Holmes Hummel, who was a former lead professor at what was then called the School of Earth, Energy and Environmental Sciences at Stanford University and was the top advisor on climate policy to the Obama administration. So while I didn't go to Stanford, I did get my hands on a copy of the curriculum of their earth sciences and other engineering programs; not only that, but I got direct mentorship from the person who wrote the book.

Working for the Indigenous Environmental Network has probably defined my life as a man up to this point. When I began to work with them, I was still very much a boy. During the twelve-plus years that I spent with IEN, I saw my father pass on to Creator, I had two sons with my wife Koren, I saw two administrations of

President Bush and Vice-President Dick Cheney and, in Canada, the fall of the Liberal Party and the rise of the Conservative right-wing fascist party. More directly, I had the opportunity to work with hundreds of communities and tens of thousands of people who were affected and assisted by our work.

Tom Goldtooth did a lot of things for me. He welcomed me into his home, into his sweat lodge. He even put me out on the hill on my fast. He taught me about the sacred journey, the beauty path. Our work at the Indigenous Environmental Network took us all around the world. I worked on the UN Framework Convention on Climate Change, the UN Commission on Sustainable Development, and the UN Permanent Forum on Indigenous Issues. The whole way, I had Tom guiding me. All of my work with IEN— all the relationships that I made, with the Black Mesa Water Coalition, with Ponca, with REDOIL in Alaska, all that work supporting these communities, winning, losing, losing, winning, losing, learning about the elements of our cosmology and world-view that all Indigenous Peoples share, not just in Turtle Island but all around the world—was preparing me for the biggest fight I was going to get into, at least so far.

The first time I went to the Alberta tar sands, it changed my life.

I was six years into my twelve-year service as a campaigner with IEN. And from that moment, my work for IEN was dedicated to fighting the monster that is the tar sands, figuring out how to strangle it, how to starve it—but also how to do that in a way that not only lifts up the communities impacted by this insanity but also makes sure that the workers are taken care of. The tar sands is the biggest employer of Native people in Canada, and following quickly behind it are the mining companies. Our people become dependent on these industries; they profit off their own demise. They are held hostage to the companies that rob them. We need to stop the companies. But we also have to save the hostages.

The activists and communities I'd met over the years are my brothers and sisters. Their struggle will always be my struggle. But the plains of the Navajo is not my land. The jungle of Chiapas is not my land. The forbidding Arctic is not where my ancestors lived and hunted. The land means everything to my people. There is no distinction between my being and the soul of the Earth and trees and water. I had been angry for years by the time I took my place in the fight against the tar sands. Injustice makes anyone angry. But the violation of the tar sands is not just injustice. It was personal.

The plundering of the bitumen beneath the forest floor is one of the greatest acts of violence against the sacredness of Mother Earth I had ever seen. It is as severe as the acts of violence perpetrated against our Native women and girls every day. Just like the anger I felt when I was younger and heard about the legacy of murders of Native women landowners by greedy white men in Oklahoma, when I went to the tar sands I got angry. I got angry seeing the hundreds of square kilometres of boreal forest that had been bulldozed, the irreplaceable complexity of ecosystems scraped away. In just one day of operations in the tar sands, industry moves enough earth to fill the Toronto SkyDome to the roof, and they do that twenty-four hours a day, 365 days a year. They have moved more earth in the tar sands than was moved by the Great Wall of China, the Suez Canal, the Pyramids of Giza, and the world's ten-largest earthen dams combined. The network of wastewater tailings is so vast that from the International Space Station, it looks like lakes. Industry refers to all the teeming biosphere they destroy "overburden." To them it is garbage.

Because of the energy intensity of the extraction operations, every barrel of oil produced at the tar sands results in the poisoning of four to six barrels of pristine fresh water from the Athabasca River. The tar sands are made up of a thick, dense form of petroleum called bitumen mixed with 90 percent clay, sand, and water. In order to separate the bitumen from these other components, vast amounts of natural gas are used to heat water, which is then added to the mixture, and this process blasts the bitumen out of the sand. The water is recycled, but when it has become too toxic, it is dumped into a series of lagoons that cover an area amassing 170 square kilometres and growing. These are not tailings "ponds"; they are toxic inland seas. Every single day, these tailings ponds leach 11 million litres into the Athabasca River and into local groundwater sources. Add that up over 365 days a year and you end up with a catastrophic *Exxon Valdez*– or Gulf of Mexico–style oil spill flowing down the Athabasca River and straight into Fort Chipewyan—every single year.

Fort Chipewyan, home of the Athabasca Chipewyan First Nation, the Mikisew Cree Nation, and a Métis settlement, is a fly-in village of twelve hundred people situated in one of the most epic and beautiful places on the planet, on the Athabasca Delta, right on the shore of Lake Athabasca. The Athabasca Delta is a UNESCO World Heritage Site. It is the second-largest freshwater delta on the planet. The people in that territory have subsisted off Lake Athabasca and the Athabasca River and delta since time immemorial. There are moose, beaver, berries of all kinds, and many medicines. Tens of millions of migratory bird species go there to have their babies every summer. It is essentially a grocery store for the local Dene, Cree, and Métis people, and a couple of the non-Natives who live there too.

All of this is being contaminated on a catastrophic level. I became angry when I visited the local graveyard on my first trip to northern Alberta, in 2005, with the Indigenous Environmental Network because that graveyard had way too many fresh crosses in it for a little village of twelve hundred. The trajectory of the expansion of the tar sands extraction in the previous decade directly traced a line of deaths from rare forms of cancer. There had been over a hundred deaths from cancer in Fort Chipewyan in recent years. Five of those one hundred deaths (three confirmed, two suspected) were from a rare form of bile duct cancer that has been scientifically linked, through long-term research on mammals, to exposure to polycyclic aromatic hydrocarbons over long periods, a process known as bioaccumulation. That toxin moves up through the food chain, from micro-organisms to smaller animals and to top predator species. In northern Alberta and other Indigenous territories, the top predator is humans.

Fishermen are coming back more and more frequently with mutated fish, with huge tumours. Hunted moose and caribou are being left out in the bush because when cut open, their meat smells sour or is yellow and full of tumours. Ducks and geese feathers smell of oil and are coated with oil. When hunters pull muskrat or beaver apart, the animals smell of petroleum. Or hunters find these little critters, which are usually pretty damn good to eat, already dead, with bleeding noses, poisoned. All because of the massive contamination, on a regional scale, downstream from the tar sands.

The government of Alberta undertook a health study and found that people in Fort Chip had elevated cancer rates—30 percent compared with the provincial average. The Provincial government gave themselves five years to respond to their own report, and that was in 2009. At that time, the medical practitioner in Fort Chipewyan, a brave doctor from Ireland, John O'Connor, was witnessing these rare forms of cancers and he blew the whistle. Rather than responding to this credible practitioner who had worked in the community for years, both the Alberta and the federal ministries of health tried to discredit O'Connor and take away his medical licence. But Dr. O'Connor was a tough scrapper and he ended up vindicated, though at a great cost. It aged him, his whole family, and the people who care about him. Dr. O'Connor kept talking and telling his story, not just in Canada but also in Europe and the United States. An award-winning documentary, *Living Downstream*, features his story and has helped the average Canadian and American relate to the human rights situation in a racialized community in northern Canada and become politicized on the issue. This is the power of narrative-based storytelling.

And it's not just the wildlife that is treated like "overburden." I had not witnessed such incredible poverty, homelessness, and drug abuse like I saw in Fort McMurray, in the street, out in the open, since my time living in Vancouver observing the Downtown Eastside. The difference between the Downtown Eastside and Fort McMurray is that in Fort Mac it's minus sixty in the winter. Workers rent out the backs of cars to sleep in at $100 a night. The average cost for a seven-hundred-square-foot one-bedroom apartment in Fort McMurray is between $2,000 and $3,000.

Twenty years ago, Fort Mac had a population of 30,000. It has the infrastructure to support 35,000 citizens. Today more than 108,000 people live in Fort McMurray, predominantly white males between the ages of eighteen and forty-five. There are approximately six men for every woman in that city. In Fort Mac, pimps bring Indigenous girls, some as young as twelve, into the work camps, and security turns a blind eye.

All of this is part of a boomtown economy. This economic paradigm that comes with mega-resource extraction dispropor-tionately affects women—from staying in dysfunctional and abusive relationships because they can't afford places of their own, to the overrepresentation of men in high-paying jobs in the industry. There should be an entirely new designation of home-lessness in the western provinces for the single moms who stay in abusive relationships because they can't afford a place for their kids and themselves in Fort McMurray, Edmonton, Calgary, Regina, Saskatoon, Fort St. John, or Prince George. The eco-nomic distortion that is the fallout of trillions of dollars of devel-opment in northern Alberta reaches into midwestern Canada and to the coast of British Columbia.

The tar sands extraction has grown much bigger in the past ten years. But our fight and our resistance have grown much bigger too. Through our work at the Indigenous Environmental Network, we were able to support the Dene, Cree, and Métis people affected by the tar sands. We were able to build up the most visible and powerful climate justice and Indigenous rights campaign in human history. We figured out that the goal of industry and government was to get a pipeline built to the coast so they could sell oil on the international market to the highest bidder.

Driven and guided by the powerful testimony of Indigenous women from Fort Chipewyan who had been fighting against the tar sands for decades, we started to organize the fight against the largest construction project in the history of humanity.

No one is helpless. No matter how mismatched the fight, the underdog always has some advantage she can use (and I say "she" deliberately; it's always the women who first take up the challenge). Even remote First Nations living in the midst of the tar sands development—staring down billions in international capital, a government that had a centuries-old history of mistreatment, and an army of bulldozers and dump trucks the size of prehistoric beasts— had to have *some* leverage. We just had to figure out what it was.

The clues had been staring us in the face for years. From Brazil to Oklahoma, from Nebraska to Alaska, extractive mega-projects need the machinery of colonialism. They divide and conquer, because they need to. The social divisions within Native communities are not an unfortunate side effect of colonialism. The way Native men and women become addicted to the jobs provided by energy companies, just as their brothers and sisters become addicted to booze and crime, is not incidental to colonialism. It *is* colonialism. That's because the colonists and extractive industries need us. They need our acquiescence.

That was our leverage.

In Canada, Indigenous Peoples have a powerful legal regime, through constitutional protection of their treaty rights to hunt, fish, and trap. The reason oil companies love to slap their logos on Native projects is that they know we hold the key to their vaults. Our treaties protect our rights. And our lawyers and activists protect those treaties.

The strategy we settled on was what we called a "rights and title campaign." We would assert our rights to our territories. We figured that if we started to choke-hold these pipelines, we could keep the tar sands landlocked. Oil that can't get to market is worth less. If it's worth less, the return on investment of tar sands projects drops. And it's no secret that tar sands oil is a high-cost, low-margin investment to begin with. We realized that we could make it a much, much worse investment.

Since those pipelines were heading to refineries south of the border, I organized the first trip of funders and heads of the major national environmental organizations in the United States, and they saw tar sands as a credible way to lubricate the ushering in of a climate change policy in the United States. IEN understood that if we channelled resources to First Nations to support a multipronged strategy of legal interventions in the courts and on-the-ground organizing rooted in ceremony, leading towards mass mobilization, we could eventually defeat Big Oil. We call this the Native rights–based strategic and tactical framework.

At that time, the white environmental organizations in the funding world were uninterested in human rights and were focused exclusively on the climate. So we had a tough go at first. Not all division within the movement is sown by oil giants. I had some powerful people shout at me in front of other powerful people, telling me that my strategy and tactics, and specifically working in partnership with the Aboriginal legal regime, were not effective. Everyone has their own ideas, and every one of them comes with some level of risk. We were attacking the Death Star. There wasn't much room for error. But we stuck to our plan.

We worked with community leaders from the Mikisew Cree Nation, Athabasca Chipewyan First Nation, and probably a dozen other First Nations from British Columbia, southwestern Ontario (where Enbridge was building its Line 9 crude oil pipeline), and the Lower 48 (where TransCanada's proposed Keystone XL pipeline would be part of a massive pipeline from Alberta to Texas).

In the last forty years, there hasn't been a major environmental campaign won in Canada without Indigenous Peoples playing a significant leadership role. Through the concerted effort of organizing community-based action camps, we taught grassroots community members a baseline of campaign skills to have greater success in their efforts. The legitimacy of Indigenous legal challenges led by tribal councils, tribal governments, and First Nations governments to go into the courts and challenge Canada constitutionally, using our treaties and inherent rights, have had a proven track record. In 2008, the Beaver Lake Cree Nation launched the first-ever constitutional challenge against the Canadian government, the Province of Alberta, and about twenty mining companies for the illegal sale of nineteen thousand tar sands leases on their traditional land. Their argument is that their treaty right to hunt, fish, and trap is being compromised by the encroachment of a toxic industry that destroys the habitat of the animals they subsist upon. When they win that case, it'll make those nineteen thousand oil and gas leases in their homelands illegal. It'll send shock waves through investment markets globally, and dozens of other First Nations will launch similar cases using that precedent.

The basis of the Native rights–based approach is the fact that in Canada we live under British common law, which is all about precedent. The reason our First Nations haven't used our treaties in Canadian courts is because no one nation wanted to establish a legal precedent that would have a broad range of implications on all First Nations people if they were to lose the case. You set a bad precedent on treaty rights, you're screwed for a long time. But with rock-solid cases where we can demonstrate ecocide and a detrimental impact on constitutionally enshrined and protected treaty rights, the tables have turned.

We knew that we had to organize beyond communities in the

tar sands. We knew we had to bring together a great many brig burning white-hot fires of resistance across Canada—everyday Indigenous people and community activists getting together and taking action. What resulted was the creation of a network called Defenders of the Land, which is the organization that founded Indigenous Sovereignty Week in Canada. Today, Indigenous Sovereignty Week is held in about eight countries and eighty cities. Activities include weeklong decolonization and colonial education curriculum workshops in universities all across Turtle Island and beyond. All of this work was done with very little money.

We won a lot of battles. We moved the most powerful leader in the Western world, President Barack Obama, to reject the northern segment of the Keystone XL pipeline in the name of climate change, in the name of Indigenous rights. (The southern segment, from Oklahoma to Texas, had already been built.) We persuaded the highest office in the United States government, the most powerful military superpower on the planet, to say no to Big Oil for the first time. When we beat the Keystone XL pipeline, President Obama made a visit to Standing Rock, to the home of Sitting Bull. While there he met with young people and he made a lot of promises to those young people about the climate crisis and responding to it while addressing the rights of Indigenous Peoples. (Promises that have since been broken.)

All the infrastructure that was built up to get in a ditch fight with President Obama and TransCanada Corporation was transitioned into the fight against the Dakota Access Pipeline. The Dakota Access fight became one of the biggest mobilizations in the contemporary history of Indigenous Peoples.

Now that the standoff at Standing Rock has come to an end, the spirit of that resistance has been dispersed, and many of the old people are now saying that Standing Rock is everywhere. The arrogance and mean-spiritedness of Donald Trump is exemplified in his resurrection of the Keystone XL project. Those who participated in Standing Rock turned their attention to the attempts of TransCanada and the US administration to ram through that project. Tens of thousands signed "a pledge to protect" the water and land of the Lakota people and committed to travelling to the construction zones to commit civil disobedience if TransCanada ever renewed construction on the northern segment. A month after President Obama rejected Keystone XL, Donald Trump brought the project back through a presidential executive order, and the fight continued. But on Joe Biden's first day in office, the new American president reversed Trump's decision and effectively killed the KeystoneXL project forever.

When I started with the tar sands campaign, there was about $50,000 of direct community funding, out of a multi-million-dollar pot. This money was designated by multiple foundations in both the United States and Canada and was administered by one central group. Today there's close to $3 million in direct community funding—lots of it goes into lawsuits for First Nations. Things have changed as a result of the sophistication of grassroots community activists who have been able to leverage support from their tactical allies, the traditional NGO world, and unconventional organizations such as the Indigenous Environmental Network in order to internationalize their struggle.

To put pressure on the Canadian economy, we knew that we had to take the tar sands struggle to Wall Street; we had to take it to Congress; we had to take it to Europe. We began to organize campaigns targeting European banking institutions, investment management funds, the managers of the big multi-billion-dollar union funds, and some of the biggest pension funds on the planet, like CalPERS, the California public employees pension fund. We knew we had to target legislators as well as big markets where Canada might want to sell its dirty oil—like the European Union, like the US Congress, like California—and encourage them to be leaders in the climate policy fight. First Nations from Fort Chipewyan and other communities asked the European Union

to adopt strict standards on fuel quality and to strictly govern—
and ban—high-carbon intensity crude oils like dirty tar sands, if
not for the lives of people dying downstream, then for the lives
of millions across the world who are being affected right now by
catastrophic climate change and by food insecurity, water insecurity, and many associated issues.

We got traction. We engaged some of the biggest operators
in the tar sands. First Nations people talked to the banks that
lend them money and told them flat out, "This is a risky, risky,
risky investment. There are too many risks and liabilities associated with investing in an unstable investment climate. Project
stoppages and delays due to litigations of Native people asserting
their Aboriginal rights and title will lead to millions, if not billions, of dollars in costs, affecting your bottom line." The case
studies are there to prove it. In Canada, for the last forty years, no
environmental victory has been won without First Nations
people at the helm. For the most part, when major environmental victories occur, on the front line all the way to the Supreme
Court of Canada, it is due to the assertion of rights and title of
Indigenous people with the support of other social movements,
such as the environmental movement and their invocation of
Canada's environmental protection laws in the courts. When we
look at massive victories like stopping the James Bay mega-hydro
proposal in the 1980s and the Mackenzie Valley Pipeline project
in the 1970s, it was an Indigenous rights-based strategic framework that turned the tide. However the support of non-Native
allies did play a part. In the next decade, Alberta will be forced to
phase out the tar sands and a big reason for this is that Indigenous
people in Alberta will continue to assert their rights as the first
people of this land.

By the time I got involved in the tar sands fight, I was battle-
hardened. That's the other element of what Tom Goldtooth
taught me: how to be a warrior. He taught me how to make hard

decisions. He showed me how to go into a situation so that I could extract information from our adversaries, those who would stand against the rights of Mother Earth, and how to talk straight to our community people, how to create unity. There is power in solidarity. Tom taught me how not to be seduced by power, how not to glorify it, how to respect it.

But it is not always wise to be hard, even for a warrior. Hardness can make you insensitive to the very things you're fighting for. A famous philosopher warned that you have to choose your enemies wisely, because that's who you will resemble most.

I was angry. I was hard.

But how can you not become hard when you're faced with tragedy wherever you look? I saw violence and broken lives when I looked around downtown Winnipeg. I saw communities systematically robbed all over Turtle Island. I saw the land itself raped and plundered. Who wouldn't be angry?

But anger is a dangerous fuel. It consumes you even as it nourishes you. It enslaves you, just as oil companies shackle communities to the industries that destroy them. I could not go on forever scorched by anger. Activism is dangerous work in that sense. And there were so many times when the dark elements of this work took me to dark places.

nîpîy

———

ᖨᐧᐱᑊ

———

water

y mom did a good job raising me. She always worked, even when she was going to school. She would always make sure that I had food to eat. There were times when I'd be visiting the rest of my family and food was scarce and somehow someone would scratch together money to get flour and lard and baking powder and make bannock. Grandma or my mom or one of my aunties would bust out some jam. My cousins and I would have been running around in Central Park or somewhere in the North End and, not having eaten all day, two or three fresh-baked bannocks would disappear in minutes.

I have lots of memories of bannock and tea when I was a kid, either in the inner city or out on the trapline in Jetait. My mom would make campfire bannock. Or my great-grandfather Edward Hart would—and he could use only one arm, so seeing him make bannock was quite impressive. He had gotten polio when he was a kid, and it had crippled one of his legs and one of his arms. His one good arm was sinewy with strength. He could do anything with that arm. He'd put his rifle on his forearm and shoot and he was a damn good shot. He was a phenomenal hunter, trapper, and bannock maker.

There are a lot of amazing stories about Great-grandpa Edward. Both my great-grandparents were medicine people. They were a bush pharmacy. I remember men coming out of the bush carrying cuts of moosemeat or bottles of whiskey to trade with my great-grandparents for traditional medicine. My great-grandparents were powerful people, in the sense that they carried a powerful spiritual force.

There is one story that has been handed down, not only in our family but throughout the community. One day my great-grandfather Edward was in his canoe and an evil force started to pull him to shore, like a current in the water. On the shore was a Wi'tigo, a human possessed by the Winter Spirit.

The Wi'tigo is something we Cree do not often talk about openly, but I believe it is important, so I will explain. We do not believe in evil the way Christians do. We know that darkness is not something that just inhabits the underworld. It lurks in all of us, and it is dangerous to nurture it. The most horrifying threat comes not from the darkness of the forest but from the darkness of our hearts.

We associate this darkness with the winter because the winter is a time of scarcity. There may not be enough for everyone. It is a time when we are tested by privation, when we are tempted to set aside our concern for those around us and turn against them. It is in these moments that we are tempted to surrender to a consuming selfishness. From allowing your appetite to turn you against those you are meant to nurture, it is only a short step to cannibalism. After all, if taking food meant for another means they will starve, you might as well be eating them.

The rapacity of the Wi'tigo knows no bounds. Nothing will satisfy it. It will eat its family. It will even eat its own fingers and lips. Only the strongest can avoid being consumed by the Winter Spirit. Our people are not afraid of wolves, but we fear the Wi'tigo.

The current drew my great-grandfather relentlessly towards the shore. He could see the Wi'tigo had eaten its own lips and fingertips. My great-grandfather tried to shoot him, but his gun jammed. Still the canoe was tugged towards the shore. When he reached the bank, my great-grandfather had to fight the Wi'tigo with the butt of his gun. He fought the Winter Spirit hand to hand. He defeated the Wi'tigo that day, but his hair turned white and he was sick in bed all that summer.

This story marks my great-grandfather as a warrior. He

grappled with the spirit of nihilism, and he won. Darkness and madness laid a trap for him, and he found a way to triumph. Why did the Wi'tigo attack him that day? I believe the answer to that question is that the Wi'tigo lies in wait for all of us. All of us have to be strong enough to resist the spirit of rapacity and self-ishness that will steal from us our sense of purpose and our sense of responsibility to those we should nourish and nurture.

There are forces in the world that do not show up in head-lines or spreadsheets. We do not often mention them in our accounts of history or our five-year plans. But we must take them seriously, and fight their corrupting influence. Otherwise we will become their servants.

Like all Natives, I have been deeply affected by residential school. For more than one hundred years, Indian residential schools were part of settler-colonial state policy.

My mom went to church-run residential school. My biological father went there. All my aunties and uncles. My grandparents. All my older siblings. My auntie Lisa, my uncle Ovide, and I were the first people in my family to not go to residential school. Everybody else in my family went to Indian residential school. The state took them away from their families and put them into government-sanctioned, church-run residential schools to be assimilated into Canadian society and have the Indian perma-nently erased from them.

But my family suffered more sadism on top of that. My father lost his virginity to a nun. My mother had to stay awake at night, hoping to protect her little sisters from predators. Though I have never been in a residential school, through my family I know the darkness that was bred there: the terror of each night, the reek of urine in the dormitories from all the scared kids peeing their beds.

We don't believe in evil. So what is the name for the horror that engulfed generations of Native kids?

My mother is a deeply spiritual person. Prayer is an important part of her life, and believing in a higher power is a big part of the narrative that she has told me throughout my life. She talks to Creator to protect me when I'm out in the world, when I'm not in her arms: "Creator is watching over you, my boy," she says. So from a very young age, Indian spirituality was a core of my being. My mother did her best to expose me to pow wow culture, the occasional sweat lodge or pipe ceremony, and often would burn sweetgrass and sage with me.

She shared with me the importance of talking to Creator and our ancestors through prayer, and the act of prayer over the years morphed back and forth between Christian style and our own traditional style in our Cree language. She was always very dedicated to telling me stories about my great-grandparents, who were revered medicine people, and any time there was trouble, she would be quick to remind me that we had powerful spiritual protection that stemmed from the prophecy, offerings, and ceremonies my great-great-grandfather George Nicolas had made. I was lucky to have had that connection with the culture of my people.

But even I was cut off from traditions as they had been handed down generation to generation through time immemorial. I was cut off because I was cut off from the land. But I was also cut off because those who should have been able to hand it down to me had had it stolen from them.

That happened deliberately. It was not an accident of history, like other crimes and tragedies. It was a policy.

Canada's first prime minister, Sir John A. Macdonald, who was superintendent-general of Indian affairs when the government enacted the residential school policy, said:

> When the school is on the reserve the child lives with its parents, who are savages; he is surrounded by savages, and though he may learn to read and write his habits, and training and mode of thought are Indian. He is simply a

savage who can read and write. It has been strongly pressed on myself, as the head of the Department, that the Indian children should be withdrawn as much as possible from the parental influence, and the only way to do that would be to put them in central training industrial schools where they will acquire the habits and modes of thought of white men.

Article II of the UN Convention on the Prevention and Punishment of the Crime of Genocide stipulates that forcibly removing children from their parents' care is an act of genocide. Of course, the United Nations and the ethical norms it came to embody did not exist in the mid-nineteenth century. The word *genocide* didn't even exist. And people had very different ideas about raising kids than we do today. White people did, anyway. In 2017, a mass grave was discovered on the grounds of a former orphanage in Scotland, revealing systematic abuse and cruelty. Similar graves have been found in Ireland. That the abuse of Native kids was not unique does not make it any less monstrous. What it shows is that you don't *have* to be a racist to be monstrous. We can be hideously cruel and even sadistic, all while convincing ourselves that we are doing *good*.

It may not be helpful to judge the architects of the residential school system by today's standards. They claimed to be taking Indigenous children from their parents and cauterizing their connection to their language and culture for the kids' own good. Maybe that was so. Maybe they weren't truly bad people. I believe in my heart that many wanted to do the right thing. But then how do we understand a tragedy so complete, so long-lasting, that it matches the definition of genocide? How does one commit a crime of historical scale without even meaning to?

I think that is much more dangerous than bigotry. That is the Winter Spirit. That is the greatest threat. That is what we all have to be wary of. We all need to be warriors like my great-grandfather.

I graduated with top honours from Medicine Fire Lodge. As encouragement, the program offered a government-sponsored bursary for $2,500, which was quite a chunk of money to a youngster like me. To get it, I had to attend a Sundance for four days in Saugeen First Nation and I had to deliver a community development project of my own in the community I came from, in my case, the inner city of Winnipeg. I thought: *Hell yeah, I'll go to a Sundance!*

My mother, through her own healing process, embraced various forms of Christianity throughout her life. She never went to Catholic church, aside from attending Catholic-run residential schools as a child, but she always believed in the teachings of the Bible and the words of Jesus, and so I also attended churches. As an older youth, I started to get into trouble a lot, like a lot of young Native men do, especially young Native men who don't have their dads in their lives. So my mom spun the globe of churches, and when I was nine or ten I ended up getting baptized and attending the Church of Jesus Christ of Latter-day Saints for quite some time. I was never going to be a Mormon. Mormons call Natives "Lamanites." They think we're not quite as good as they are. But while it was a very racist experience, there was some good to it. When I was baptized in that church, I felt Creator touch me. A wind blew over my face. It was a profound moment.

I have always believed in Creator. Whether I was doing it in a Christian way or doing it in our Cree way, I've never had a problem talking to God. I always believe that my great-grandmother and especially my great-grandfather are guiding me and protecting me from any harm. Although I had a pretty crazy youth, with a lot of violence, a lot of substance abuse, and a lot of emotional trauma, I survived it—in part from being inspired by my mother's resiliency as a residential school survivor and a single parent who was the first in our family to acquire not one but three university degrees and a registered psychiatric nursing diploma. She did her

best to instill in me a deep sense of connection to my cultural practices and Indigenous cosmology and worldview.

It would be impossible to understand the thrill of ceremony
for us without remembering that for generations most of it was
deliberately suppressed. Across Turtle Island, our traditions of
potlatch and Sundance, our songs and drums and traditions,
were outlawed.

Many survived in disguise. I remember the tea-box dances in
Puk as a kid. Our ceremonial gift-giving was illegal, but square
dancing was not, so families would spend months preparing traditional gifts, which they would pack up into tea boxes. Then
they would dress up in their moosehide regalia and spend the
night dancing and exchanging gifts. In ways like this, my people
managed to keep the ember of tradition burning secretly.

But imagine what it would be like having your traditions torn
from you, disgraced and outlawed. Imagine your own most dearly
cherished traditions—say, Christmas. Now imagine that one day, in
your childhood, you were snatched away from your family, suppos-
edly for your own good, and forbidden from celebrating Christmas
ever again. No stockings or carols, no trees or presents, no turkeys.
Certainly no mass. And no English. And especially no joy, no
Christmas spirit, no fellowship, no sense that everything is OK.

Would that change you?

Now imagine trying to recreate all that, years later, from the
words of a grandparent. Instead of simply inhabiting your traditions, you would be relearning them. Rediscovering them. Even
when you had them back, though, they would not be the same. It
would be a sweet relief to have them back. You might cherish them
all the more. But you would be forever haunted by the years you
had wandered through life without the meaning they offer.

Joy, lingering grief, pride, relief. All these converge as we
reclaim our traditions. We are still picking up the pieces. But
they are making us stronger, more whole.

———

A sweat lodge is the most fundamental ceremony of the First Nations. It is a purification ceremony, the process by which we cleanse ourselves of our failures to walk in the way we have promised ourselves and our communities that we will walk. It is our chance to shed anger and fear, to atone for misdeeds and thoughts and emotions that harm ourselves and others. It is a chance to pray for what is right. It marks a momentary return to innocence.

I'd already gone to a few sweats with young people from the Native Youth Movement. A sweat lodge looks like a womb, and that is what it is. When you pull up the flap that covers the entrance, you enter the heat and darkness. A drum beats gently, echoing the mother's heartbeat that marks the first months of life. That is why the drum is sacred to us.

Rocks have been heated in fire, and glow. We call them "grandfathers," because they have been on the Earth long enough to have seen and heard everything. We honour them, because they become sacred once they have been heated. They can be used only once. They give up their spirits to nourish ours, so we thank them.

The Elder splashes water on the rocks, filling the lodge with vapour that surrounds the participants like amniotic fluid. Taking turns, we pray for each other. We pray for release from our guilt. We pray for the well-being of loved ones. We pray for strength. And we suffer. More water is splashed after each prayer, and the small dome becomes punishingly hot. We emerge refreshed.

As a teenager, I needed more than my fair share of refreshing. The inside of a sweat lodge is a world away from a Warriors' drug house or the inside of a detention centre. And yet, perhaps not so different. Over the years, I have met some pretty hard cases inside a sweat lodge. And I have met some good men in bad places too. But what the sweat marks is the moment when you *want* to be clean. When you set aside your weakness and corruption. If only for a few hours, wanting to be clean and being clean are the same thing. The sweat lodge realigns us with what we know to be right, even if we are not strong enough to walk that way every hour of the day.

A Sundance is a path or a way of life that one follows. It is much more than a ceremony. Although your responsibilities to the Sundance way of life change over the years, every time the Sundance ceremony comes around again, it signals the Cree New Year, in the way that January 1 marks the start of the new year for the moniyaw, or white man.

I was so excited for my first Sundance. When we got there, the organizers said to everybody, "Who here has smoked pot or drunk alcohol in the last few days?" I put my hand up and they asked, "When did you do it?" I said, "Two days ago." They said, "Well, you can't go in the lodge until Saturday. You can help out around the lodge, though." Everybody else was drinking and smoking the night before but they didn't speak up and they just went into the lodge. Over those first few days, I listened to the Sundance, the sounds of the eagle whistles and the drum, and people praying. I felt like a loser sitting outside the lodge.

The morning that I was allowed to go into the Sundance lodge, I got up bright and early. As I walked towards the lodge, I heard the drum. When it's time for the dancers to get up and sing, the drummers give them a warning drumbeat. They hit the drum four times. They do it slowly and powerfully. I heard: *Boom. Boom. Boom. Boom.* Then I heard a Cree song that means "Thunderbird, come into the lodge." The person who sang it was a well-known singer named Alfred. He was leading that drum. I was completely moved. I remember thinking: *I want to do that. I want to sing that beautifully.*

Then the drums slowly started up, and the whistles of all the dancers kicked in. It's a chirping sound. *Chu chu chu chu.* The sun was just starting to come up and the whole scene was indescribably beautiful.

Perception is a weird thing, not just for an Indian, but for all human beings. Here I was at the ceremony that we've been doing for thousands of years. It felt familiar to me, though I'd never seen anything like it. I felt humble, and I felt the exhilaration of being part of something bigger than me, bigger than this moment.

The person I thought was in charge was cutting a man's chest and stuffing pegs into his flesh. Even that did not seem out of place to me.

He wasn't a Sundance chief, though. That cutman, Ralph Kent, ended up becoming quite a significant figure in my life. I went up to him and I said, "Yeah, hey. How you doing, man? Yeah, my name is Clayton. I'm from Winnipeg. You look totally busy there, cutting and everything. But this is my first time coming to a Sundance and, you know, maybe later you'll have some time and we could sit down somewhere and have some coffee and you can tell me everything there is to know about the Sundance. I'd sure love that."

He looked at me like I was crazy and he started laughing. He put his hand on my shoulder and he said, "I'll tell you what. I don't have time to go and have a coffee with you. But if you find yourself not doing anything, then go around and ask people if they need help until somebody puts you to work. You get that work done. Then you do the same damn thing until you are too tired to walk anymore and then you go to sleep. When you get up tomorrow, you do the same thing all over again. OK?"

I said, "OK." I went around and asked people if they needed help. I've never chopped so much wood in my life. When Sundancers need to go use the washroom, they get someone to dance in their place. I did that and I managed to get a name out of it.

When I was two years old, my mother took me to Long Plain First Nation, where I was given my spirit name, my clan, and my spirit colours by the late George Daniels, who was a highly respected Anishinaabe Elder. A spirit name is an important part of how Creator, our ancestors from the spirit world, and spiritual helpers recognize us. They don't recognize us by our Christian name. I had always had that childhood spirit name that I got when I was a baby, but I didn't have a man name.

Some of the helpers at Sundance heard I didn't have a name, and at that time I didn't remember what my childhood name was and I didn't know what my clan was and I didn't have my colours—all the things that someone who lives a Sundance way of life has. So they said, "Oh, go up to the tree, they are giving names right now." As if I was going into a 7-Eleven to pick up Tostitos.

I went up to the centre tree in the Sundance Lodge. There was an old man, Gerald, at the tree. He is a well-known painter and a really good healer in the region, although he stopped doing that healing work many years ago. Gerald later became my friend. He had only one eye. He put his hand on me and he touched the tree with his eagle fan and crunched his face, and his one eye was looking all crazy and manic and he said, in his really deep voice, "Hmm. Hmm. Zhoon Gay Binesay Anini. Strong Thunderbird Man . . . Oh. Same clan as me. Kinew. Eagle clan. Yeah. OK." He also gave me my colours. That was it. I felt this huge surge of energy go through me and fill every part of my body. I looked down and I was covered from head to toe in mud and dirt. I was the dirtiest person in the lodge. I'd been working so hard I hadn't even paid attention to my appearance.

I left the lodge, thinking: *I'm Strong Thunderbird Man. Holy cow.* Bullets couldn't penetrate me at that point. I was walking down the trail and there was that cutman, Ralph Kent. He was walking with a cigarette hanging out of his mouth. He had wispy, ratty-looking hair, Fu Manchu facial hair. He looked like a lynx. It turns out he was Lynx clan. I walked up to him and I said, "Hey man! I took your advice. Holy shit. Best advice ever. I worked my ass off and I got my name. I got my spirit name and I got my clan."

His cigarette had ash hanging off it and he said, "Hmm. Hmm. Well that's good. That's good. I'll give you one more teaching, OK?"

I said, "Yeah, sure!"

With the index finger of his right hand he poked me right in my chest plate. So hard that it hurt. He said, all ominous, "Now you know better." The ash on his cigarette didn't fall off. He walked away. I thought: *What the fuck was that all about?*

I didn't know until a week or two later, when all the spiritual high of the experience started to wear off. I was at Wellington's, underneath the St. Charles Hotel, for Techno Thursday. I was lifting up a Black Ice or some shitty beer I drank at the time. I went to put it up to my mouth, and for the first time, I heard my helpers say, "Nah. You don't want to do that."

The more I drank, the louder those voices got. Talking to me. Reminding me about my experience at the Sundance. The songs I had heard grew louder and louder the drunker I got. At that moment, I felt my chest hurt a little and I remembered Ralph saying, "Now you know better."

The Sundance ceremony is a four-day ceremony that begins first and foremost with the harvesting of a Grandmother Tree, a white poplar. This is the tree that holds up the lodge, entirely made out of poplar trees tied together with rope made from willow bark. In the way I was taught the Sundance represents the transference of the teachings of the Thunder Beings to humankind. The lodge is eight-sided and faces south. Men dance in the west. Women dance in the east. The drum and the pipes sit in the north, and the sacred fire sits in the south. In the top of the tree of life that resides at the centre of Sundance Lodge is a handmade eagle's nest and in it a tobacco offering containing the prayers of all attendees of the Sundance. This is the offering to the Thunder Beings.

To be a Sundancer is to humble yourself. Dancers, men and women, give up their food and water for the duration of the four-day ceremony, offering it instead to your ancestors. They dance through the day and the night. You sleep outside, on the ground. You wouldn't believe how hungry and thirsty you are, how you sink down in exhaustion.

While they dance, they blow their eagle whistles, made from the bone of the eagle, which is symbolic of the hungry cries of a baby Thunderbird. The Thunder Beings respond to the offerings of the tobacco and the calling chirp of the eagle whistles and the dancers' sacrifice of food and water by providing guidance, healing, and protection and the teachings of the Sundance way of life.

Offerings of flesh through various forms of piercing happen at the Sundance, but only if a dancer has been given a vision through his or her dreams. The only thing that is truly yours is your flesh, so flesh is the holiest offering. It is given up in a spirit of humility. The Elder measures off a span of flesh on your chest with an eagle talon and marks it with ochre. Then you lie down on a buffalo hide and pray. You are consumed with thirst, and faint with exhaustion, but your mind is completely focused on the prayers that have honed your mind and spirit to a fine point over the last three days. Thinking about the past. Thinking about the future. Thinking about what you want to make right.

When the cutman pierces you and inserts a piece of wood through the strap of flesh on your chest, the feeling is one of relief. Not pain.

Then a rope connects you to the Thunderbird's tree. You dance backwards four times. On the fourth you keep going, until either the rope or the strap of flesh gives way.

You are warned to pray carefully, because your prayers will be answered. Don't pray for stupid things. Everything I have ever accomplished began as a prayer on that buffalo hide.

What happens at the Sundance is a microcosm reflection of what will happen over your year. One of the golden rules is that whatever you put into Sundance in terms of sacrifice and suffering, you will get back in blessings throughout your year. I have now been going to Sundance for twenty-two years. Sundance is my reset button, my opportunity to atone for all my mistakes in the year and to get right with Creator and what is best about myself and what has been wounded over the years.

Sundance had been my first time going to a ceremony, learning about Indians who weren't hyper-masculine or hyper-angry or hyper-dysfunctional; sober Indians working from a centre of unconditional love, with the objective of healing. That's what I saw at Sundance.

Although the nations that live in Turtle Island are as different from each other as Greeks and Englishmen, Germans and Spaniards, the purification ceremony is something they have in common. I was once invited to a sweat lodge on the east coast, far from the lands of the Cree.

The Passamaquoddy, who are relatives south of the Mi'kmaw Nation in Nova Scotia and New Brunswick, live in what is now called Maine. A liquid natural gas company was trying to build a massive liquefied natural gas terminal on a sacred site called Split Rock, in the Bay of Fundy on the Atlantic Ocean, a place where whales swim and where the Passamaquoddy had been gathering for generations. I supported a group of grandmas who were trying to save their sacred site. I stayed with an old Passamaquoddy Elder, who had a sweat lodge and a little trailer right on the Bay of Fundy, who told me the story of the Wabanaki Confederacy and the big drums. He had noticed that when I had introduced myself it was in the Midewiwin way, the Ojibwe way. It's all Ojibwes in Winnipeg, so I learned how to pray in Ojibwe, not in my own language, Cree. This old man said, "I'll do a sweat lodge for you, if you sing for me in that sweat lodge and you sing all Ojibwe songs because Ojibwe is a sister tongue to Passamaquoddy. It's the same language and I can understand you and the spirits will understand you. You will make them happy." Mi'kmaw, Ojibwe, Potawatomi, and Passamaquoddy are all part of the Algonquian language family, and the words are similar. So he did a sweat for me and we prayed that we would stop that liquid natural gas terminal.

When the sweat was over and we came to the fourth door, we opened the door and a snowstorm had started. Half the sky was covered in stars and there was a full moon. There were grey clouds with light snow blowing sideways and a cold Atlantic wind blowing in. I was butt-naked because it was just him and me. Then it was as if Creator or Grandfather pushed me—I marched down to the Atlantic Ocean and I dove in. I opened my eyes underwater, and because of the moonlight, I could see clear as day. It was a blue moon and it lit up everything under the water, and I could see the black Atlantic rocks beneath me. I could feel that spirit of the Bay of Fundy, the Atlantic Ocean. It was less feminine than the Pacific Ocean; it was strong in a different way, colder. Then the cold came like knives into my lungs because it was the Bay of Fundy in November in a snowstorm. I lost my breath, and I had to stand up. I tried to take a breath, but I couldn't breathe. Finally I was able to catch my breath and I walked out of the water and ran into the house and had the best sleep I'd ever had.

When I was in Oaxaca we were invited to go into a sweat lodge with an old grandma. Because I had just been at my first Sundance, going to this spiritual ceremonial place was something that I took very seriously. Their sweat lodges are in a big brick oven, like a cabin, with red, red heat. A little fire burns in the back and you take all your clothes off and you go in naked. The medicine woman gives you a bunch of medicine wrapped up into a ball. Before you go in, they do body work on you. They find your sickness with their hands. With me she stuck her hands into my stomach, into my solar plexus, and I could feel her touching my spine through my stomach, and through the translator, she said, "Your biggest sickness is the ball of anger that you carry deep inside you. You need to get that out." Then we went into the sweat. While she sang songs, we were supposed to hit the place where she'd said there was sickness.

This old grandma humbled herself in front of us and went in naked, so I decided that I was going to do the same thing. The other Winnipeggers were cracking jokes. I remember being in that sweat and telling my friend Richard and Larry's nephew to smarten up and have some respect. Right there in the sweat, Richard threatened to punch my lights out. Richard and I were best friends before that. But we were never friends again. And I never saw Larry's nephew again after we turned back from Oaxaca.

When I got back to Winnipeg from Oaxaca, I went to go see an old man for help in removing some of my anger.

I haven't mentioned my anger much, because I didn't notice it for many years, no more than a fish notices water. Anger was the medium I moved in. Anger seduced me into conflict with every authority figure I crossed paths with. Anger lured me into crime. It made senseless violence and pointless destruction the only way I could express myself. It made drug dealing and prostitution seem justified. Because if nothing matters, anything goes. That is the corrosive tide of nihilism.

And when I found the path of the land warrior, I only became angrier. Injustice is gasoline on the fire of anger, and I burned. I burned bright sometimes, and I got shit done. But I burned those around me. And I was burning myself up. Anger was my sinew. Anger was my fists. Anger made my voice crackle with dangerous energy when I spoke. Anger is rapacious. It consumed me, like the Winter Spirit. I had to free myself.

We went through some sweats and ceremony. He gave me a smudge called anger medicine and I smudged with that for a whole year. It was amazing how much less I swore during public presentations after a year of smudging with anger medicine. But it is not easy to let anger ebb away.

There is no way that we, the First Nations of this land, can fight without understanding what we are fighting *for*. There are those who say the ends justify the means. That is not what I am saying at all. What I am saying is that the ends and the means are bound together, like the heat and the grandfathers that glow in the sweat lodge. Our Native way of life calls upon us to live our lives upright. It calls upon us to speak the truth. It calls upon us to be courageous, even when courage is difficult to find. We do not walk this path because it gives us an advantage. We walk this path because the wisdom of millennia has taught us that this is the right way to live in this world. It is the right way to honour this world.

When I was working in the Navajo Nation, I heard the stories from the old people and from the young people I was travelling with. I had the opportunity to meet David Johns, a widely known Indigenous Diné abstract artist. When I was staying at his house in Winslow, Arizona, I said, "I love stories, and when I travel, I collect stories. Can you tell me stories about this part of the world?" He said, "Yes, I can." I thought it was just going to be a quick coffee chat in the morning, but we spent the whole day talking.

He talked about the Rainbow Road from the other universe that the Diné travelled to come to this world, which they call the Glimmer World. He talked about the great beasts, huge monsters that used to terrorize the people. He talked about the changing woman who gave birth to the hero twins. The hero twins were armed with weapons from earth and they defeated the beasts. To this day when you drive through Navajo, the mesas— with red earth spilling out from the tops—are the bodies of the beasts that the hero twins slayed, and towering Shiprock is where they had their fight. It is the remnants of the monsters that the hero twins cast away so that the people could live and thrive.

That is a very crude interpretation of a beautiful story that David Johns shared with me. After that journey, every single journey that I went on, whether it was to Oklahoma, North Dakota, Fort Berthold Three Affiliated Tribes Indian Reservation, or the Alberta tar sands, I made sure to not just learn about the fight that the Native people were going through. I made sure to learn about the cosmology, about the worldview, about their connection to the sacredness of the place where Creator put them so that I could, in my best way, in my best understanding, support their organizing in a framework that came from the way they see the world.

Throughout that process, I worked with Tom Goldtooth and Heather Milton-Lightning and other people in IEN, and all of us, in our own way, embraced the pipe. We embraced the Sundance way of life. We embraced the sweat lodge. We embraced fasting. We embraced what the Navajo call the beauty path, the beauty way. The Navajo believe that everything should be beautiful. Whenever you pray, whenever you make something, whenever you take action, you should make it as beautiful as you possibly can so that you honour our ancestors. The spirits like colour. They like beauty. They like cleanliness. They like beautiful singing. In Navajo, I learned that when you pray, great thought and effort and attention is put into speaking very eloquently and articulating thoughts in a beautiful and clear way. That's how you honour the spirits.

The beautiful part about working with IEN and working for Tom and all of the Elders on the IEN board and in the communities that we work with is the very strong spiritual foundation. My work with IEN was always guided by Spirit, by Creator. I learned from Tom that when you do this work, you have to never stop talking to Creator. Even when you fall, even when you have moments of weakness, you must always talk to Creator. I was able to navigate through some pretty hairy moments and come out on top. I was able to enter into corporate boardrooms and stare CEOs right in the eye and tell them, "You're not going to hurt our people anymore. We're going to stop you. Creator is going to help us." It always felt good to see these rich old predominantly white men shake in their boots in the presence of grandmas from Navajo Nation, or the Gwich'in Nation, or any of the other nations. It was very empowering to witness our people speaking for themselves—not some slick environmental NGO from Washington, DC, or Vancouver or

Ottawa but grassroots Native people in the halls of power, on Wall Street, on Bay Street, at Capitol Hill, at Parliament Hill.

There is no way of learning the way of the warrior without learning about love. I was lucky that love came to me when I most needed to learn how to live my life right.

At my first Sundance, I was welcomed into the Eagle clan. Each of the clans carries a teaching and a strength. Ours is unconditional love. The eagle sees farthest and flies highest. That is what love gives us. Without it, you cannot soar. Without it, you are blind. You can see what is true only through eyes you share with the beloved.

I have been with Koren, my wife, since 1995. I love Koren. I have dropped everything for Koren, multiple times. I would quit the movement for her. We've been through a lot. We've been best friends for twenty-plus years.

The first time I saw her, I thought: *I want to spend my whole life with you.* I was seventeen and had just gotten out of juvie. I had moved back to Winnipeg and I'd had a hard winter. I'd been expelled from school again, and my mom had told me that if I wasn't working or going to school, I couldn't live with her. So I took off. I went to downtown. I was floating around and being transient, trying to find my identity. I was staying in a friend's place in Osborne Village, in an old mental hospital that had been converted into an apartment block in Osborne Village, a trendy neighbourhood that was a lot nicer than the West End or Central, where I would work. The old hospital was widely known to be haunted. I would hustle at night, do whatever I could to survive—doing scores and trying to sell whatever I could get my hands on, sometimes drugs, sometimes stolen goods, stolen electronics, anything with monetary value. Back then it was VCRs, CDs, VHS movies, that kind of stuff.

Because I only worked at night, I had the daytime to myself. I would hang in what these days would be referred to as a hipster café, the Roasting House, in Osborne Village. Going there was an escape for me, a chance to see some culture. To many Winnipeggers, the Roasting House was an iconic place where a lot of relationships began and ended. It was a place to see and be seen. I used to sit at the Roasting House and contemplate life.

One day shortly after Christmas in 1994, I was sitting there with my good friend John Gold. I used to always get Irish Cream coffee. I don't know why. I can't drink that shit anymore. The fake oil flavour rots my gut. But back then I loved it. I took a sip of my coffee and I looked up—and it was like the scene out of *Wayne's World* when Wayne sees the woman he is interested in and time slows down and that 1970s love ballad "Dream Weaver" comes on and there are sparkles all around the screen. There she was. Koren. The most beautiful woman I had ever seen. I zinged. She was wearing a vintage oxblood leather jacket with a leather belt and a pair of tight-fitting blue jeans and fancy leather gloves and had a little patent leather purse. She had very thick hair, dyed red red red, just past her shoulders. She was opening the door and she swung her head and her hair went swoosh and swung around. She lifted her purse, and I remember I zoomed in on her fingers in the fancy gloves, holding the leather purse.

The whole thing took my breath away. I elbowed my bro beside me and I said, "Do you see that woman?" My bro made some kind of crude remark. I said, "Hey hey. I'm serious here. You see her?" He said, "Yeah, yeah, I see her, man." I said to him, "It may take me a year, it may take me two years, maybe three years, but that woman is going to be my wife." He made another dumb remark, but he just kind of faded out. Everything faded out. All I saw was her walking out of the Roasting House, going down the stairs onto Osborne Street and then disappearing.

Being an immature seventeen-year-old who'd never learned how to treat a woman properly, instead of thinking that I should

just introduce myself, I came up with an elaborate scheme to get
to know her. I started seeing her at the café in the after-school
hours. She would always leave before five o'clock, before sup-
pertime, I assumed to catch a bus home. I started finding myself
there at the exact time, all the time. She had this friend who I
wasn't as attracted to and so I found her a lot less intimidating.
I got it in my head: *I'll approach this less intimidating person and
get to know her, and then maybe she'll start talking about me to her
friend*. I was thinking that then maybe Koren would be interested. It was ridiculous. Nowadays, I think I would just say,
"How are you doing? I'm Clayton. Can I buy you a coffee?"
Anyway, I talked to her girlfriend, Gaby. Sure enough, Gaby
told Koren that I said hi to her.

A little while later, I was walking down the street in Osborne
Village and I ran into Gaby and Koren at a bus stop. Gaby said,
"Hey Clay, how you doing?"

I said, "Hey Gaby, how are you doing? Good to see you. Who
is your friend?"

She said, "Oh, this is my girlfriend Koren. We grew up
together."

Again everything faded away. I zoomed in on Koren. I said,
"Koren, eh? Really nice to meet you."

Koren was, of course, real sweet to me and really shy and she
said, "Yeah, nice to meet you too."

Right away I said to Gaby, "Thank you for introducing me
to Koren, Gaby." Then I just focused on Koren and I said, "Do
you want to go for a tea?"

She said, "What do you mean? Where do you want to go?"

I said, "Let's go over to the Country Time Donuts."

I was just getting into the rave scene. I was wearing a long
black trench coat. I had my fingernails painted with some MAC
beauty product. I was wearing concealer and mascara because I
was a little bit queer/androgynous. I looked like trench coat
Mafia or some shit. We walked over to the coffee shop and sat

down. I said, "It's nice to meet you. I see you at the Roasting House all the time." I remember she commented on my rings and my nail polish and I remember I bragged, "This is MAC colour blah blah blah." It was insane how beautiful she was—how beautiful she still is. My heart was beating through my chest. I was sitting there and I wanted to hold her hand so badly.

After that, we got to know each other a little better. I'd see her at the Roasting House and I'd buy her a coffee after school. I quickly learned that she had very strict Baptist parents, who came from a Mennonite background. She had to be home by dinnertime every day. They never let her out at night. She couldn't go to raves, couldn't go to clubs. She was sixteen, so she was underage. I knew that I wasn't going to be able to be with her for a while so I committed to just getting to know her. I would buy her her favourite cigarettes, Benson & Hedges Menthol. I would say, "Here's some cigarettes for school. D'you want some lunch money for school?" She'd say, "OK, give me some lunch money." I'd buy her coffee, or whatever she wanted.

Then the Roasting House closed down, literally overnight. I didn't have any way to meet her. I didn't have her phone number. I didn't know anything about her flight path. Nothing. At that time I was getting in deep with my brothers, doing what I had to do to get by. Months passed, and come the springtime—May 11, 1995, to be exact—I had a platonic date with a girlfriend named Lara. Lara was a shining star, a drama queen. She was often in plays and she was an incredible actor and a really amazing person to talk to. I didn't know that she knew Koren. Koren had been hanging out with her the day before and she'd said, "Oh man, I'm feeling blue." Lara asked why, and Koren said, "Well, there's this guy that I knew. This Native guy. Clay. And he's nowhere to be found. We used to see each other at the Roasting House, then the Roasting House closed down and I don't know where he is anymore. I haven't seen him in months." So Lara said, "Clayton Thomas-Müller? I got a date with Clayton tomorrow! Why don't I cancel with him and tell him I've got to go do this play, and you go out with him instead."

I was at home just chilling and the phone rang. As soon as I heard her voice I knew it was Koren. She said, "Hi. I'm not sure if you remember me, but this is Koren."

I said, "Of course I remember you."

She said, "Oh, OK, cool. It's been a long time."

I said, "It sure has. Do you want to hang out today?"

She agreed and I ran out the door and my brother John and my uncle Brian had just pulled up in their big Thunderbird. I didn't have any money, so I rolled up to my brother John and I yelled, "Dude! Dude! Dude! This woman called! Money! I need money! Give me some money!"

He said, "Holy fuck. Take it easy there, bro. OK, sure, here." He gave me forty bucks.

I said, "I need some fucking weed. Now."

He said, "Fuck, OK. Here, man," and he gave me a bag of weed. He said, "Geez, you better fucking get lucky. You just broke the bank on me there, bro." But I was already running down the street.

We met up at a place called Zine's Magazines, one of the first internet cafés in Winnipeg. You could get cheesecake and a latte and surf the net. They had fancy magazines from around the world. There she was, looking incredibly beautiful. She had a flowing slim-fitting blouse that showed her shoulders and her collar bones, and Doc Marten boots and coffee-coloured lipstick. She was smiling. I sat down and I said, "Can I get you a dessert?" and she said, "Yeah." I got us strawberry cheesecake to share and a couple cappuccinos.

And it was awkward. It was awkward as fuck. Finally, I said, "Hey, do you smoke pot?"

She said, "Yeah. I do."

I said, "Why don't we go out back, smoke some pot, come back in here, and try this again."

She said, "Yeah, OK, that sounds good."

I told the woman behind the counter, "Hey, we just have to go outside for a minute. We're gonna leave our cappuccinos and our cheesecake here and we'll be right back."

We rolled out to the back lane. We smoked like two grams of the craziest weed right there in a little pocket pipe I had and got wrecked. Then we went back in and had the best conversation ever. Koren said, "You want to go for a walk?" We walked to the Legislative Building and we looked at the black star, an optical illusion, in the middle of the building. We admired all the marble carvings and found ourselves on the third floor looking down into the rotunda, and at that moment I kissed her. I was so shy that I couldn't kiss on the lips. I kissed her on the neck and soon we were passionately making out. I told her flat out, "I've been think-ing about you since I last saw you. I have not stopped thinking about you." She said the same. We walked across the street to the park on Memorial Drive. At the time there was a famous pool there that was surrounded with cedar bushes. We went into the bushes and we ended up snagging.

Then as quickly as the date had begun, it ended. I walked her to the bus stop and I said, "I want to see you more."

She said, "My parents are very strict. They are very religious. I'll try to see you when I can. It's always got to be in the daytime, though."

I said, "OK. That's no problem. I'll see you whenever I can see you."

We began to see each other, though not exclusively. She was always my girl on the side and I was always her boy on the side. We both went on living our regular lives. At the time I was selling drugs for the Manitoba Warriors. I was running a drug house and working late hours. She was going to high school with a 4.0 GPA and was a Royal Conservatory grade 10 pianist. She was white. I wasn't. So yeah, unconditional love had something to do with it. We wouldn't have got far without it, because there were landmines around us everywhere. But I'm Eagle clan.

The first time I met her parents, I was standing outside their house. I was helping Koren move out. She was moving in with me. The meeting was tense and cold, but her mother called me up soon after. She was freaking out. Koren would get pregnant, she said. She would never go to university. Her life would be ruined by me.

I said, "Elanore, Koren is a leader. She will go to university. She'll be fine, I promise you."

Her mother calmed down, and I was right. Koren *is* a leader.

Faith is a hard thing to grasp sometimes. I remember when I was a little organizer—back when I was a lot slimmer—I was heading up to Poplar River First Nation, on Lake Winnipegosis, to talk to some young people. To get to the Poplar River, you've got to drive over the winter freeway. They bulldoze from the shoreline onto the ice to create a road. There are trees lined up on either side of the bulldozer, but it's ice underneath your tires. I was driving my mom's Hyundai Accent, which all my friends called the Little Green Machine. I don't know what happened, but it conked out right when I got to the ice. This old-timer I knew, Neil Hall, saw me. He was a singer, and a cutman at Sundances. Neil would give me lessons every time I hung out with him. Every now and then I could sit at their drum and sing with him and his sons. They're all good singers. Neil saw me and he said, "Well, you should still come to the youth conference even though your car's buggered up. I'll give you a ride."

I said, "Are you crazy? I can't leave my mom's car here."

He said, "Don't worry. As soon as we get back, that thing'll start up like nothing was wrong. Just have faith."

I said, "OK, right, whatever." We went to the youth conference and I was real happy that I went. Sure enough, after the conference, when we drove up to the Little Green Machine at the edge of the ice of Lake Winnipegosis, it started up without a complaint. Neil looked at me, gave me a friendly chuckle, and went on his way.

When I started to reconnect with my culture and get my shit together as a young man, after I had gotten out of Manitoba Warriors and learned how to organize in the inner city, I found that the weekends were hard. All my friends were really into partying. In becoming woke, I didn't want to party. I would hitchhike out to Brokenhead Ojibway Nation to see the Elder Ralph Kent, who was the cutman at my first Sundance. Ralph was a mystical, complicated character. He had served time in prison and I'm pretty sure he went to residential school. He was a real rough-around-the-edges Elder, and would travel from Sundance to Sundance teaching people how to pierce, how to cut. He was also a badass hunter. He could shoot three bucks running at five hundred metres. Ralph was one of a group of Elders who had learned under the Anishinaabe Elder Herman Atkinson.

For many years, I was part of the crew of young men who gravitated towards Ralph to learn some of his teachings. When we'd be out on Brokenhead, Ralph would put us to work, cutting or stacking wood or pulling nets out of the lake, chopping up the fish, helping clean out the ceremonial grounds, or setting up the sweat fire. His wife, Glenda, would feed us a big bowl of deer liver for breakfast, with bannock and strong coffee, and Ralph would drag us out in waist-deep snow. To go get firewood we'd have to go into the forest.

Every weekend—if you paid attention—he'd drop some crazy teaching. The things we would do were very much like Jedi School. We used to fast together, all of us at that lodge. Ralph had a grandfather water drum and a little boy water drum—two important tools that you use in the Midewiwin lodge for winter, spring, fall, and summer ceremonies. You make a big lodge out of willow. You've got a fire in the middle, and you have people all around. The water drum sits on the west side of the lodge, and the entrance to the lodge is in the east. The north side of the lodge is where the women sit, and the south side is where the men sit. We would do our fasts in that lodge and receive the teachings of the grandfather water drum. Ralph could shape-shift. I remember being in a sweat lodge with him one time and I opened the door and he looked at me and he still looked like a lynx, pišiw, which was his clan.

Ralph liked to swear a lot. He'd even swear in the sweat lodge. But at that time in my life when I was young and trying to get out of gang life, the fast life with drugs and alcohol, I needed a hard teacher who could be very strict with me. Ralph would say, "If you're going to fucking fast, then fucking fast." No half measures.

He was always warring with other lodges and getting into fights with other medicine people. But I have also seen him heal a lot of people. Ralph has a comprehensive knowledge of medicine and ceremony. My great-auntie Caroline, who is the matriarch of our family, has gone to see him for many years for medicine for her stomach. Over twenty-five years ago the doctors told her she had just weeks to live from aggressive stomach cancer. But because of Indian medicine, she is still with us today. I always had respect for Ralph Kent.

I danced for three years at Ralph Kent's Sundance, but I always felt like the odd man out. There were two brothers that Ralph would always dote over. They were hard-working big guys from East Selkirk, from the Métis settlement. Ralph would give them eagle fans and pipes and teach them about the different ceremonies. Ralph would never do shit for me. I had a pipe but somebody in the city had given it to me. I had an eagle fan, but only because nobody claimed it after it was left at a pow wow that I had organized.

I was about to enter my fourth and last year of my four-year Sundance commitment at Ralph Kent's lodge. My brothers

Stewart and Brennan and I had all learned how to sing, and some of the other boys in our Sundance crew seemed to resent that we could sing. At the winter Sundance meeting, in front of all the Sundancers, they accused us of being egotistical and thinking we were better singers than them. There that day was Walter Benes, a friend of Ralph's and one of the most respected and well-known Sundance men and singers, who'd been going to Sundance since the 1920s. After we had been scolded, Walter got up and he walked over to the drum and he said to me, "I feel sorry for you boys. Never in sixty years of Sundancing"—or maybe he said eighty years, whatever the hell long-ass time of Sundancing—"have I ever seen such pitiful boys. You are not good singers. You have a lot to learn." He said, "I'm going to leave now. And I'm never going to come back here ever again." In front of all the dancers, he left.

When Walter walked out, Ralph lost his temper. He started swearing at me and my bros, saying that we had big fucking heads. My bro Stu almost got in a physical fight with Ralph and the boys. Stu's hotheaded and he started to provoke Ralph in his own lodge. He said, "Oh yeah? You're powerful, all right. You're the most powerful medicine man on Earth. Not." We had to leave because I had my kid sister with me, and she was only six years old. Ralph's other helpers escorted us to our vehicles. I looked at Ralph and I said, "Ralph. You need to stop this. I have a child here." He kind of came to his senses. He said to Stewart and my other bros, "Get the fuck out of here. Don't you ever fucking come back." He looked at me and he said, "You can go too if you fucking want to." I left and that was the last time I saw him for almost twenty years. I've always regretted that we had a falling-out.

During one of our four-day fasts, when we were all hungry and thirsty, Ralph said to us boys: "OK, I want you all to be aware of your dreams. We're going to talk about them. We're going to learn to interpret dreams." Ralph could interpret dreams. I was very excited about this skill of learning how to interpret dreams.

The next day he asked, "So what did everybody dream?" People were telling what they'd dreamt. I had dreamt about Ralph and Glenda and their children. They were inside their sweat lodge and everything around the sweat lodge was on fire. The trees. The grass. Everything. But they were safe inside their sweat. I shared that dream, and everybody in the lodge got really upset with me, including Ralph. They said, "You're a fucking sicko, Clayton. What the fuck is wrong? You're really screwed up." They told me my dream was indicative of how messed up I was in the head.

But a couple years later, when I was in my early twenties and had moved from Winnipeg to California, I got word that there had been a gas leak and that Ralph Kent's entire house had filled up with gas and there had been an explosion. Their house was badly damaged. I think a pet may have been killed. But Ralph and Glenda and their children were safe.

Recently I was given the opportunity to see Ralph and Glenda at Turtle Lodge. Saugeen elder Dave Courchene was part of a big campaign to stop the Energy East pipeline. He was working with my organization, 350.org, and the Lummi Nation to bring a totem pole, a powerful spiritual emblem of their nation, to place in the pathway of the proposed pipeline.

When the totem pole arrived to Winnipeg, we organized a massive welcoming march of the sacred object that had travelled across Turtle Island, from Washington State, through the mass protests at Standing Rock. After we marched the totem pole with five thousand people through the streets of Winnipeg, we brought it to Dave's lodge to be raised in the pathway of the proposed pipeline as a powerful symbol of Indigenous resistance of the mega-project. Ralph came down to see what all the hubbub was about. It was by the sacred fire that I ran into him and Glenda after many years of not speaking. He had lost both legs from diabetes. He was still funny as shit. I asked him, "Are you still running Sundance?" He said "Yep. Yep. Sweat lodge too. Except for now, I swing like a fucking monkey when I'm doctoring in the lodge. " It was nice to get a chance to talk to him again after many years.

A Sundance wedding is a ceremony that fuses your spirits together for eternity, so your marriage is not just a mortal relationship but an eternal one. As part of a Sundance wedding, a man has to go hunt on his wedding morning and bring something back for his wife to cook for their first meal together. Before you go on your hunt, you have to light a fire, and you get only one match. If it doesn't light with that one match, you have to wait another year until you can marry.

So on the morning of his wedding, my bro Brennan was pretty stressed. After he lit the fire, he and I got a .22 and we went out hunting. Brennan didn't have his glasses with him and he is blind without his glasses. He couldn't shoot a thing. We ran into my brother John, so he came with us and he said, "Well, fuck, why do you have to shoot something? We'll just grab one of these boats and go out on the lake and grab a fish. That should be easy enough. We'll catch you twenty fish." We went out on the lake with John and rode around the lake all day long and we didn't catch shit. We showed back up and the entire Sundance lodge was waiting and they'd thought we were going to be gone for ten minutes. We almost showed up empty-handed, but then one of my aunties gave Brennan a goose, so he was able to marry that year.

I didn't have to kill a goose when I got married.

After five years together, Koren and I got engaged. She had changed my life. She had helped push me out of the Manitoba Warriors. I needed someone like that. Sometimes love is a kick in the ass. Koren had watched me take my first steps on my journey towards activism. She had seen me learn, or relearn, the wisdom of the Native traditions that would free me. There was no way I could imagine myself without her.

The pressures of our engagement and undercurrents of racial tension with her family triggered my fight or flight. I choose flight and ended up connecting with another woman, and Koren and I decided to live apart. She got her own place and I continued to pay her rent, pay her bills and my own bills, which led to a circumstance where I slipped back into selling drugs on the side while being a teacher for at-risk Native kids.

When you tell a story from beginning to end, it is tempting to try to force it to make sense. But that is a form of lying. I would like to be able to say that I had learned my lesson, that I had put crime behind me, that I had the strength to lead others. But I was a hypocrite. I lied to myself and others then, but I can't lie now. I was seduced by the easy way.

Then I got the shitty news that she was seeing another guy.

I had recently travelled to California, and while I was there I was offered a job coordinating an organization called the Indigenous and non-Indigenous Youth Alliance, which was based out of the San Francisco Bay Area.

I was burned out doing all frontline work. I saw a lot of young Native people die or end up in jail or just disappear from the Indigenous rights movement. At the same time, I got word that three distant cousins of mine from Pukatawagan had all committed suicide. We have a suicide epidemic in First Nations that has just gotten worse. Younger and younger kids are killing themselves. A lot of our young Native people start out proud to be Native, and then they face the realities of systemic and interpersonal racism and they are shamed. They get hurt by our broken family structures. They come to a reckoning in their adult life when they have the power to control what happens to them. Some succeed, but many don't. They end up in the prison-industrial complex or dead.

About a week after I heard that my cousins had committed suicide, I went down to visit my aunt Rhona. I had lived with my auntie Rhona when I was a teenager, after my mom kicked me out of her house. My auntie Rhona was very loving towards me. As a teenager, when I was still involved with the Manitoba Warriors, her husband, Ken, was one of my best friends. My auntie Rhona let me live with her in exchange for babysitting. But living with her, I saw first-hand the struggles of my cousins and everything that comes with living in poverty.

At one point, my mom hadn't heard from my auntie Rhona for a couple days. Everybody was trying to get ahold of her and I said I'd go to her house and check on the kids. When I got to the house, the door was open. I went in and there was my baby cousin, Thunder, who had been left alone. There were dishes everywhere. It looked like somebody had started a bonfire in the living room. I snapped. I thought: *I'm getting out of here, away from Winnipeg. I have no power to do anything here. I've got to go or it's going to drag me down with it.*

I resigned from Anishinaabe Oway-Ishi. I got it in my head that I was going to persuade Koren to come with me to California. We weren't really talking and I followed her one day as she was getting on a bus to go to work. I drove up all dramatically and I asked her point-blank, "Do you love this guy?" She said no. I said, "I love you and I think I deserve at least one chance to give it another shot. I'm moving to California. Come with me. If you like it, stay, and we'll get married. If you don't like it, I'll get you a ticket back to Winnipeg. Six months. No questions asked. You can tell everybody you lived in California." She told me that I had thirty days to get us to California, or else. I said, "Thirty days, or what?" She said, "You don't fucking want to know." Then she got on the bus and went to work.

When Koren and I arrived in the Bay Area, it was two weeks after 9/11. Military Humvees with .50-calibre machine guns were driving over the Golden Gate Bridge, and marines carrying M16s patrolled the Bay Area Rapid Transit stations. Every single public washroom in America was closed, and we were exposed to a heightened level of militarization, paranoia, and Islamophobia.

We went through that experience in a city that most activists and leftist academics refer to as the Bubble, where the 1960s free love movement started, where the Black Panthers started, where the American Indian Movement occupied Alcatraz and began the longest walk to Washington, DC, in the '60s and '70s. There's a lot of rich history there and many historic landmarks, from People's Park in Berkeley to the Golden Gate Bridge in San Francisco, all in one megacity by the Bay.

That first year Koren and I were in California was difficult. We both ate a lot of beans and rice and Tapatío hot sauce. But by 2002, we were both finding success. One day, after a year of living in the Bay, Koren proposed to me. Of course I said yes. I asked her, "When do you want to get married?" She said, "Tomorrow." The next day I got her a dress and she got me a dress shirt. We went down to Alameda County Courthouse and were married. Her boss at the time, who owned Cafe De La Paz in Berkeley, had a white Jeep Cherokee, and immediately after we got married, we drove down Highway 1 in the Jeep and had a fancy seafood dinner overlooking the ocean.

Essentially from that point on, I've been with Koren. Really, ever since May 11, 1995, I've been tied to my wife. She's my soulmate. Right from the first time I saw her, in Osborne Village, and every other time after that, including this morning when she went to work, I look at her with so much adoration and so much love. Especially now that she is the mother of our sons.

Koren Lenore Thomas-Müller is the greatest thing that ever happened to me. She's the reason that I've been able to become , the man I am today, because of her strength as a woman, as a caregiver, as a life provider, as a life creator. I've been inspired by her to overcome all the adversity, all the sexual and physical and emotional and spiritual abuse that I went through growing up Native in Winnipeg. My wife, Koren, gave me the strength to survive and to build something more beautiful to end all those negative cycles. I love you, baby.

About my sixth year of working with IEN, and after experiencing many victories and many setbacks, I got the news that my biological father, Peter Sinclair Sr., was dying. I was in Washington, DC, at the time. I was living in a tent, occupying a park. I remember I was with Sarah James, a noted Elder from the Gwich'in Nation, on the steps of the Smithsonian's National Museum of the American Indian, when my phone rang. It was my brother Johnny. He said, "Dad's in the hospital. I don't know how long he's going to be here. His liver is going. You better make your way here if you want to say goodbye to the old man." I flew to Winnipeg to see my dad. We had our final words, and a couple of weeks later he passed and I travelled back to escort his body back up north.

And then my world began to crumble.

Actually, it is more accurate to say that *I* began to crumble. And I kept crumbling. I started drinking again. Whenever I had a chance, I would close the door and drink a bottle of whiskey. When I was drunk, I would do my best to get my hands on some drugs. Not just one specific drug, but really whatever the fuck I could get my hands on when the pain was too much.

I suppose that means that in all those years at Sundance, part of me had been wanting to drink all along. The Winter Spirit had been there all along. The moment I was too weak to keep fighting, it came for me. I knew the cost of what I was doing. I had seen the destruction booze and drugs bring down on those who invite them it. I knew the street kids in Winnipeg, and the way substance abuse sucked them into the traps their lives had become. My family had been torn up by booze—had torn itself up. My mother and aunties. My adopted father. The man I'd thought was my father. My real father. I should have known better.

But knowing has nothing to do with it. For some of us, there is a hole we believe only booze can fill. Most days, we will rush to our own destruction like flies to candy. We know better. We don't care. The rush of the drink you know you shouldn't take— that exhilaration is not just a chemical in a bottle. That is the relief of saying "fuck it" when the effort of holding on feels like too much to sustain.

But it's not really relief. Knowing that something is wrong and doing it all the same—that is the Winter Spirit. That is madness. That is the route to a living death. Because the guilt and sickness you feel with each lapse is just one more thing you need booze to soothe. It is hard to imagine stopping. Stopping is just going to feel worse.

But none of us is alone. Tradition and ceremony are ways to walk with our ancestors. And the love that binds us to those around us is a strength I will forever be grateful for.

One of the things that turned me around was the death of my uncle Ken, who died when he was about forty-five. After he died, I thought about all the times when I had gone to his ex-wife's, my auntie Rhona's, house. After she and Uncle Ken broke up, she had a really hard time, and it affected her kids in ways that I can't describe. It was hard for me to see her suffer and to see her kids suffer because I had lived with them for many years. I was powerless to help my family, to help these kids all around me who were being neglected because their parents were dealing with their own trauma. That powerlessness had driven me out of Winnipeg; my uncle Ken's death brought me back.

Literally a month before my uncle Ken died, my uncle Jimmy died. He died a horrible death too. Uncle Jimmy was my mom's best friend. He was a very loving man who came into my life when I was young, at the time that my mother was separating from Roddy. He would go out drinking with my mom and keep an eye on her and keep her safe. Jimmy had had polio as a kid, and his arm and his leg were crippled, just like my great-grandfather Edward Hart. He bought me my first Nintendo and he'd take me to movies. And though he was only a young man, twenty-two or twenty-three when I was a youngster, he was one of the first really positive male influences in my life. He drank a lot, but he was a kind-hearted man. He didn't have any kids and he loved me like a son.

Jimmy promised to take me to see the WWF when they came to the Keystone Centre in Brandon. I was so excited because the

Ultimate Warrior was going to wrestle. The Ultimate Warrior was this roided-out wrestler—I don't know if he was Native or not, but he was as big as Hulk Hogan and he had war paint and ribbons around his massive arms and he was fighting Randy "Macho Man" Savage for the world championship at the humble little ring in Brandon.

The Ultimate Warrior came out, shook the ropes, and did his Ultimate Warrior thing. He was praying to Creator, or someone, and flexing his muscles. To me, as a kid in the 1980s, that was a big deal. I was figuring out that wrestling was fake—I'd say, "It doesn't really look like he's hitting him, Uncle." My uncle would reply, "He's hitting him. He's hitting him. Don't you worry. He's gonna win." And he did. The big Indian in the World Wrestling Federation was the world champion. I left so excited and I told all my friends that Ultimate Warrior was the world champion. But when WWF came on the TV, as it did once a week, Macho Man was still the world champion. Because Brandon, Manitoba, wasn't a location where they were doing an official taping, it didn't change the narrative that they broadcast on television. It was a pretty grim awakening for an eight-year-old to come to terms with the fact that wrestling was kind of a weird, kinked-out soap opera.

Uncle Jimmy was always there for me when I was growing up. So when he died, it was rough. I had avoided him for a lot of years because he gave me tough love when I was living on the streets. He wouldn't give me money and we got distant with each other. Years later, we reconnected and became friends again and would chat over the phone.

His brother got killed in the inner city in a high-profile murder, and one time I was talking with Uncle Jimmy about that and I was crying, and I told him, "I'm so sorry I haven't been there for you. I just didn't know how to support you after such a fucked-up thing." At the time, he was living in hospice because he had diabetes and most of his limbs had been amputated. At one point in the call, he said, "Oh, they cut my finger off today." I told him, "Yo man, I'm gonna be back in Winnipeg soon. I'll connect with you."

I called him a week later, when I was on an airplane waiting for the plane to take off en route to Winnipeg. Somebody answered his cell phone and I said, "Who's this? Where's James?" It was his daughter. She said, "He's dead. He died a couple of days ago." Right then a flight attendant announced: "We're taking off. Turn off your phones." Holy fuck. The shock of it sent me on a spiral.

The eagle sees things clearly, and from afar. That is love. I saw the pain I brought to others with my selfishness, and how it would get worse. I saw the pain of others, and how I wanted to be strong enough to invite them to lean on me. I saw what was best in others. And through others, I saw what was best in me, what was worth salvaging from the wreck I was making of all I'd worked towards.

I needed, I saw, to actively and consciously begin to confront the post-traumatic stress that I have from growing up Indian. I started seeing a therapist in Ottawa where my family and I were living. I also began going to support groups for people with trauma and addictions. I started to talk about not just the crazy things I'd seen as a young man growing up in Winnipeg but also the trauma that I went through as a child, being sexually and physically abused. It was a very difficult time that almost caused my wife and me to divorce. I embarrassed myself in front of a lot of people that I love.

I realized I wasn't just trying to escape all of the loss: young people I had met through gang-intervention work with the Native Youth Movement and lost; my cousins who committed suicide or who had been killed in accidents. I was also running away from my mom and my auntie Rhona. What I was really searching for was exactly what I was running from—connection to my family back in Manitoba.

If I didn't sober up, I was going to lose my wife and everything I'd worked so hard to create in my career. I didn't feel I could take on the things I needed to take on without the power of my lodge in my hometown, without the strength of my spiritual base. I talked to my mom and my brother and my Sundance chief, and knew I needed to go home to confront my demons. I needed to be there in order to defeat the greed that is threatening our people and our water. I had been doing it alone for sixteen years, in California, Vancouver, and Ottawa, but I wasn't strong enough to do it by myself. I needed to surround myself with the love, care, and compassion of the people with whom I had grown up going to ceremonies. I called my brother in Winnipeg and asked him to buy me a plane ticket.

I told my wife, "I'm moving home and you can stay with me and come with me. But I gotta go home or I think I'm going to end up like my uncle." My wife had a great job in Ottawa, running an incredible catering company. It was a big career opportunity. My kids were going to the best public school in Canada, with the prime minister's kids, in Rockcliffe Park. But my wife said, "OK, let's do it. Let's go home." It ended up being a positive thing for her, too, because our kids got to have a relationship with their great-grandparents on their Mennonite side before they died, and my wife and I got to spend time with her grandparents before they died. But I'll never forget the sacrifice she was willing to make to help me become strong.

Moving back to Winnipeg has been about coming full circle. For the first time in my twenty years of going to Sundance, I was able to bring my sons and my wife with me and go through Sundance with them by my side. That in itself was worth all the suffering. I wanted to get to a place where I could provide the stability that I'd always wanted for my sons, with a healthy community of love and support. Being back in Winnipeg made that possible.

Nothing compares to the power you have when you are home. I don't know why it took me so long, when I was suffering and so lonely. In my language, Winnipeg translates into muddy or murky water. It took me forty years to realize that in the City of Dirty Water I am my strongest.

nanâtawihowin

———

ᓇᐅᐳᑕᐃᐧᐦᐅᐃᐧᐣ

———

healing

The only way to get to our trapline is by train. You take the train between Pukatawagan and Lynn Lake, Manitoba. It's Mile 121—twenty miles after the stop for our reserve. You get off in the bush and you walk down a trail and there's our cabins, our trapline.

The trains also run through Winnipeg, of course. All kinds of lines converge there. Growing up, every time I looked at the train track I would instantly be teleported to Jetait, to my family. It was the smell that took me back. It's the same stones, same smell. The railway ties and ballast rock are saturated with creosote and some kind of fire retardant. Nothing else smells like railway tracks. When I catch that scent on the wind, I am a little kid again, walking down the tracks with my cousins. The vast meadows of Jetait are filled with blueberries, raspberries, and cranberries. The laughter of other children eating campfire bannock and tea. My great-grandmother's soft hands, so full of love.

Jetait and Winnipeg feel like different worlds, and yet they're connected by these ribbons of steel. It has been that way for a long time. Steel connecting one world and another. For many Native people, the train is a power archetype, the Iron Horse. Trains brought with them colonial expansion. Each train brought more white people. The train says, "Hey, get out of the way!" When the track-laying crews arrived, those spikes might as well have been pounded into our hearts. That steel ribbon cut us off from our own past. So the train is burned into every Indian's psyche. I myself have had dreams of the Iron Horse and experienced the fear my ancestors felt in waking dreams. Blood memory of our genocide while they cleared the plains of the mighty buffalo. Our people starved. Our people had to move on.

But the train means more than that. In the north the train is an essential element of life. With colonization, trains replaced the rivers, which were the life vein of transportation and an essential food source. Our rivers in the north were all dammed. It was the trains that brought food, trains that brought loved ones home. Trains took our people away, and sometimes trains brought them home. For me, trains bring up a lot of emotions, a lot of memories, traumatic and good.

We hated the trains, and yet we would have been devastated if they had stopped. I had seen this before. I had known and loved those who hungered for the thing that weakened and killed them. It would have been impossible not to see the cost of dependence—the way it corrupts your heart and gnaws at your health and leaves you at the mercy of others.

Everything is connected. The barren train depots are connected to the spruce forests of my trapline. The urban gangsters are connected to the Elders on their traplines. The bleakness of despair is connected to hope. The way of the warrior is not for some of us to defeat others, it's not for good to defeat evil, and it's not for one idea to erase another. It is to find a path through the false choices.

In kindergarten, at Linden Lanes School, I had a teacher named Ms. Gryer, who was a cruel woman. Whenever I'd make a mistake in her class, she'd make me stand in the garbage can in the corner. She'd get all the kids to stand up and she'd say, "Why is Clayton Thomas in the trash can?" The whole class would say in unison what she'd taught them to say: "Because Clayton Thomas is garbage." I knew it was wrong but I didn't know what I could do. I was a powerless little kid. I had no way to defend myself.

I always wondered if my mind manufactured or sensationalized some of these horrible memories. But years later I ran into one of my classmates. She must have been a university student by then. She was plugged into the fight the Pimicikamak Cree were leading against Manitoba Hydro, which culminated in an occupation of the Jenpeg Generating Station in 2014. She still looked the same, and I said, "Lisa Martin?" She said, "Clayton? We went to kindergarten together, right?" She looked kind of woeful and said, "I think about you a lot." I was shocked and asked her why, and she told me, "It always disturbed me how cruel they were to you in that class."

Perhaps because of the injustice she had grown up seeing as a child, it compelled her to do the right thing as an adult and align herself with the Crees in their fight against the megaproject in Northern Manitoba. Of course, I'll never know but I like to think something good came of my awful experience. Thinking that gives me hope that even when things seem irredeemable, there is an underlying decency that we can count on. It teaches me that good can come even from cruelty if we allow it to. Many of us are provoked by the spectacle of the Winter Spirit to do good in the world. That is the way of the warrior.

In my work with the Indigenous and non-Indigenous Youth Alliance, I worked with a lot of great people. We set out to change people's lives, but of course our lives were changed as well. We changed each other, and we are indebted to each other. I would not be who I am without the strength and courage of those I worked with. I am proud to be able to say that one person whose influence helped me most started out as something close to an enemy.

When we were young, Heather Milton-Lightning and I detested being around each other. It's hard now to say why, but we did. Still, when times get rough, it would tend to be she and I who would be there in the hard moments together. Heather was always the bull moose breaking the snowpack for everyone else. So even though we didn't get along and I think I irritated her, we would always put aside our differences and I'd say, "What needs to get done?" She'd say, "Well, we've got to do this, this, and this to get that done." I'd say, "OK, let's do it." And we'd get shit done.

Heather has always been a genius, and is an OG in the movement. She's one of the most dedicated and humble warriors—Okijida, as they say in Ojibwe—that I've ever met, and I'm fiercely loyal to her. While Heather can be a hard-ass, when you are in your darkest time of need, she is the light that shows up and comes down like a furious bolt of lightning, striking away darkness and evil. I truly love Heather.

One day, when I was still a young, angry guy, Heather called. She said, "Clay, I'm organizing the North American Indigenous delegation to the World Summit on Sustainable Development in Johannesburg. The Indigenous Environmental Network is coordinating Indigenous Peoples on the front line of environmental justice battles to go to the preparatory conference in New York City. Next week, we're taking twenty Indigenous leaders to New York for the second preparatory conference. I need someone to help me out because it's too much work. Can you come and help me?"

I said, "Heck yeah, I'll come up." So I went to New York, where I'd dreamed of going since I was a boy, and I participated in a preparatory conference for the World Summit. Heather got me to speak on various expert panels about the impacts of the extraction-based economy on Indigenous culture, particularly young people.

For all of my young adult life I had been working to decolonize the generation I was part of, to help unfetter the minds of our young people from a mindset that kept them from achieving community and personal self-determination. I got kids out of gangs and into sweat lodges. I got kids out of drug houses, and out of prostitution, and out of the city. I had seen the broken lives and damaged spirits at the frontier where colonialism still tears into our culture. So I knew what I was talking about. And it made me angry. But anger is not enough if what you want is justice.

Most of the times in my life when I experienced a major shift or moment of growth, I was completely unaware that my life was about to change. There I was, deep in the bowels of the United Nations complex in New York City, on a panel of international Indigenous leaders, speaking about the issues that mattered to me the most, sharing the hard times that our Native young people were facing in inner cities across Canada. The speech I gave was my entry point into the environmental justice movement, and while I spoke I was touched by Spirit, and all the questions I had had about why it's so damn hard for us young Natives in our own homeland were answered by Spirit.

I spoke from my own experience as a kid who had seen the bush and lived in the inner city, and what I had observed in my work with youngsters who had fallen into gang life because they came straight out of the rez and had no support and English wasn't their first language and their only support system was the gang. I talked about the ones who didn't make it. I talked about the young women who ended up in the sex trade, either because of addictions or because of physical threat by gangsters. I talked about how our young Native people live in cities like Winnipeg because of the legacy of development done without consulting with Indigenous Peoples, without respecting treaty rights and inherent rights. This has created a circumstance where young Native people constitute the largest population of vulnerable youth going into gangs, like the Manitoba Warriors, Indian Posse, Deuce Knights. Mega-hydro development, the tar sands, and massive mining operations, coupled with genocidal policies like residential schools, made Native people end up in the city. Continuing that legacy in Canada, the sites where resources are, whether it's oil and gas or mega-hydro or hardrock minerals or timber or fish, tend to be in the places where Native people live. These corporations come into our homeland and destroy it. We become dispossessed from our lands and end up in urban ghettos.

I talked about how poverty has ramifications, such as the criminalization of our young people and our young people not having the same opportunities as white kids in Canada. They end up seeking out economic opportunities in the underground economy, the drug economy, the sex trade economy, the hustling and robbing economy, all so they can determine their own destiny. I talked about how I knew that the solution that would address this problem was our culture, because I myself, after having fallen through the cracks of the system, somehow managed to crawl my way all the way to the United Nations through being empowered by the Sundance way of life. I told them how, at a very young age, I'd been able to spend time with my great-grandparents at our trapline in Jetait. I had watched my great-grandfather pull fish from our nets. I had eaten rabbit stew and berries till I puked. When my great-grandparents died, my family lost connection to our land. We stopped going up north. I saw the way my family life degraded. My mom and aunties started drinking. Shit got hard.

My life could have gone in any number of directions. Maybe the odds were against me. Maybe I was more likely to stay in a world of crime and violence, of substance abuse and despair. But that wasn't my path. There are well-trodden paths that lead from self-abuse to sobriety, from victimhood to advocacy, from hopelessness to activism. And from sleeping in a bus shelter in Winnipeg to a podium in New York.

Of course there is a path from there to here. There is for everyone. There has to be, because everything is connected.

Back when I was being humiliated by my teacher at Linden Lanes, I finally released my rage. I'd like to say that I stood up to that teacher, or that I fought back against my tormentors in the schoolyard. But that's not what happened. I got my revenge on a kid named Chris. Another Native kid. He was the brownest little boy in class.

One day I was playing with a Tonka truck, one of those old-school full-steel cast dump trucks, a big one, and he took it from me. I had this overpowering fury. I thought, *I barely have anything, you ain't gonna take this little thing from me, you dirty piece of garbage.* I raged out. I picked up the dump truck and I smashed his head with it. Blood poured down his face and I got suspended. It's a big regret that I have: the one kid I made an example of in kindergarten was one of the only other Indian kids in the whole school. Chris, wherever you are, I love you.

It wasn't just me, and it wasn't just Chris. I spent a big part of my childhood, from kindergarten up to grade 5, in Brandon. Why should the Sioux and the Cree hate each other? Are they not connected, as everything is?

This rivalry and suspicion runs through almost every layer of Native life, and especially Native activism.

One of my first mentors was Rick Magnus, a white guy who ran the Aboriginal Single Window initiative, which was meant to be a one-stop shop for all things related to First Nations for any department of government. Rick took a real shine to me during my early days working at the Aboriginal Centre, where his office was. He and I would talk about the contradictions of Indigenous leadership. We'd talk about what a real leader does. He never pulled any punches. I think he was a true ally of Native folks. He really wanted to help, but I think he became disillusioned with all the fucked-up apathy and lack of drive from a lot of people, Native and non-Native, who just kept proposing the same initiatives, doing the same thing over and over, and expecting a different result. I always appreciated my conversations with Rick. I'll always remember Rick Magnus, and I know that I was able to do this work in large part because of him.

I wouldn't have learned to play the game if it hadn't been for Rick. There were a bunch of inner-city community leaders who took me in and trained me. I was good at getting money via grants, government funds, and through general hustling. But

Rick was the guy who took me under his wing. He gave me something I needed: information. I don't know why Rick chose me and why he gave me that kind of unparalleled access, but it always fucked with the Native mentors in my life because I would have information about government policy that was dropping before they did or right when they did.

Rick warned me that a lot of the opposition I was going to face would come from my own people. Mary Richard was a great community leader at the time, a very strong, fiery leader from the Métis nation. At the time, Mary was president of the Aboriginal Council of Winnipeg, which was the fiscal sponsor of my organization, Aboriginal Youth with Initiative. She always took good care of me, but I had gotten on her bad side. She sat me down in her office one day. "We've taken your files," she said. "We've locked you out of your computer. Your office door is locked. We're not going to release the last money you have in your bank account. We're terminating our relationship with you, firing you, and your project is no longer yours."

I had expected them to do that. The chair of my board, Brennan Manoakeesick, and my co-staffer, Ken Sanderson, and I had already set up another bank account and a non-profit structure. We had gotten another $60,000 grant from Rick, which we had not disclosed to the Aboriginal Council because we suspected they would set up this power play.

I told Mary, "Well, that's fine, because we've already taken duplicates of all of our files. You're more than welcome to have all of the information of the program up to this date and use it however you see fit. I have a board of directors. Brennan is the chair. We already have a new office space at the Lizzie Park Community Centre. Go ahead and do what you gotta do, but this is not the last that you'll see of me."

Mary's jaw just dropped. I remember looking at the guy at the table across from me. He had a slight smile on his face, like: *What a little bastard.*

That made me feel pretty great, but eventually I began to think about how much better things would be if all the energy we devoted to fighting each other could be directed at solving the problems we all faced. But this struggle never went away.

During my time as the executive director at Aboriginal Youth with Initiative, Phil Fontaine, the former national chief of the Assembly of First Nations, was a valued mentor in my life. The Assembly of First Nations, formerly known as the National Indian Brotherhood, is the constitutionally recognized national Aboriginal organization representing First Nations governments and their lobby agenda with the settler-colonial state of Canada. Today, under the leadership of National Chief Perry Bellegarde, for the first time in the history of the organization, it is in alignment with the conservative agenda of the government of Canada.

Phil taught me how to look four steps ahead. He is a controversial character, with his pragmatic approach to negotiating deals with the federal government. Some of the more radical sectors of Indian Country see him as a sellout. To me, he is more like an uncle who has done some crazy things but has also done some good things. The work he did as national chief, such as bringing the discourse around residential schools to the national consciousness, which resulted in the apology from the federal government, was significant. I worked with the national chief for many years as the founder of the Assembly of First Nations National Youth Council and found myself being groomed by him for politics.

During Phil's first run as national chief and his first administration, I was the national youth spokesperson of the Assembly of First Nations. I came up with strategies to get the National Youth Council off government funding so that it could become more radicalized and actually begin to address the fundamental issues that are keeping our people down. The plan was to centre on suicide prevention and gang intervention, and Aboriginal land claims and treaties, including the comprehensive land claims process and the modern-day treaty negotiation process. All of these claims were centred in extinguishment policy frameworks aimed at eliminating our unique, collective priority rights as the first peoples of this land. Things that don't get funded by the federal government.

The Assembly of First Nations thought my proposal was too radical. Phil Fontaine said, "No, you can't do that. You're going to water down our treaty rights. You are going to make our transfer payments less if you do that." He said that the transfer payments the AFN received for its bread-and-butter programming would be diminished. I said, "You could just put that government money in an account, and we'll do what we will with that. 'Cause it's the Canadian government's fiduciary and legal obligation to give us that money."

I was told by various sources that Phil had written a letter to every chief, every provincial and territorial organization in the country, that essentially said: "Don't work with this kid. He's a shit disturber." I told Phil, "You can hit me like that. You can cut me off from the Assembly of First Nations National Youth Council that I helped create. But I'm going to go away for a while and I'll come back with an independently funded network and we're going to carry on this conversation from where we left off."

Years later, here I am tangling with my old mentor. Today he runs a consulting firm that provides services for clients like TransCanada Corporation. One of the services he provides is arranging letters of accommodation from First Nations and Métis communities to lend their support to projects like the Energy East pipeline. He also worked for the Royal Bank of Canada as a special Indigenous advisor to help the bank and First Nations expand the Aboriginal market. During the time that Phil Fontaine's consulting firm was retained by TransCanada, our campaigns successfully terminated both the Keystone XL and Energy East pipelines. So I felt vindicated. Fighting the pipeline was the right thing to do. But it also felt great on a personal level, as though I had been right all along to part ways with Phil.

But that kind of victory can never be complete. It is a loss to all of us that someone of Phil's stature has diminished, just as we're worse off without Mary Richard. We should all be working together.

There are big gravel pits all around our cabins in Jetait. The gravel has lain there since the last ice age. Now there are plans to move it. A ten-lane free-trade superhighway from Nunavut all the way down to the Panama Canal is on the drawing board. And you can't build a highway without gravel. First came the Iron Horse. Now the bulldozers and excavators want to come too.

It is not hard for my family to guess what the highway's investors hope will one day travel over the ribbon made of our gravel. There is gold there too. And where there is gold, there is greed. Multinational gold-mining companies are putting pressure on all of us to give up the rights to our trapline. Manitoba Hydro and the Ministry of Infrastructure (formerly the Department of Highways and Transportation) have their own ways of leaning on us.

The easiest way to lean on us is to exploit our internal divisions. There are many in our tribal council who think they can be in both worlds at once. They think the priorities of global capital can be reconciled with the priorities of the land. But you can't be the Indian and the Iron Horse at the same time.

The result is that families are divided down the middle. Councils are divided down the middle. If you want to conquer, first divide. That is why we must remember that everything is connected.

While I have often had my differences with my fellow activists and even friends and family, and I have always been willing to fight for what I believe to be right, I have never claimed to be flawless. It has been a long road from my days of stealing cars and street fighting. And I do not want to give the impression that once I saw the right path laid out in front of me that, I never strayed off it. That path connects my accomplishments to my failures, just as the train tracks connect Jetait to Winnipeg. It was a long walk, with many stumbles.

Even when I was hanging out at the Aboriginal Centre, and the further I got away from the Manitoba Warriors, I was still not on the true path. The deeper I got into education, and this centre of Indian business in Winnipeg, the better things seemed to be. I liked hanging around with Indians trying to make a life for themselves. But I was living a duality. That's been the story of my whole life. In the daytime I'd be learning about politics and working to make the world a better place. Then I had a night life.

I continued to live a fast life. I really wanted to get out of the lifestyle, but I was still pretty buck wild. I didn't have an income, so I had to hustle when I could. I was dabbling in drug dealing and drug use. I wasn't a drug dealer, just a hustler, selling access to drugs, cutting corners and making things happen for people, benefiting from it.

I am not proud of that. I don't want to make it look glamorous. I was desperate to maintain a quality of life that all of the people around me took for granted because their parents could bail them out. I didn't have that kind of safety net. So when the going got tough, I had to compromise my morals and hustle to pay my bills and make sure the women in my life were well taken care of.

At that time in my life, I had such an interesting, complex existence to balance. I was living with my childhood sweetheart and we were making a life for ourselves. Koren and I moved out together as soon as she graduated high school and we both went on social assistance. That was how we got our first apartment together. She was quick to get a job. It was because of Koren and my brother that I left the Manitoba Warriors. She wanted me to get an education, just like my brother did, which was why I was spending all that time at the Aboriginal Centre.

It was a huge pressure because we were also teenagers and we wanted to party. One of the realities of my night life—this addiction, this safe space I found myself in at raves, after-hours clubs, gay clubs—was that these places were lacking in the thick bull-moose energy that I would often feel when hanging out and conducting drug deals with my brothers and my uncles in the Manitoba Warriors. These guys were all six-foot-plus 250-pounders who had done hard time in Stony Mountain. When you roll with a crew like that and you are just a skinny little Cree guy, you witness and are victim to the constant jockeying of all these raging bull moose who are all striving for power, to be the toughest, to be the scariest, to have the most money, to have the most power. I found the experience to be very stressful because I was always worried that some violent situation was going to explode and I would be caught in the midst of it.

I had experience with my brothers selling drugs to my people. I felt justified in selling drugs to little rich white kids in the rave scene, kids from the suburbs or River Heights. I felt that it wasn't as bad as doing it in my own Native community. Somehow I felt that I was morally free from any punishment. I felt as though participating in that world and being viewed as exotic and beautiful, being the one that brought the fun, had somehow given me a free pass because it wasn't in my community. I felt that I wasn't guilty. I did all kinds of bad things back then. I was very promiscuous. I was madly in love with Koren, but the multiple dualities I was living in my life, trying to better myself during the daytime by getting training, spending my evenings cooking dinner with my wife and beginning our life together, were often contradicted by my need to go out and have release on the dance floor, and sometimes even in other people's embrace.

I picture this time as a Venn diagram, with all of these collid-
ing universes coming together at the edges and an entirely new
particle is created where they overlap. I found myself living in a
place where I had multiple identities. I still had this persistent
identity as Clay the gangster. Then I had this identity of a young
Cree man who had come out of a very abusive family structure
trying to find my new identity and step into this new experience
of being a community leader and trying to set an example for
other young people who were going through similar experiences,
what all our mentors were calling decolonization. I was teaching
people to be sober, and I was getting high. I was helping young
people get out of that life, and I was trafficking in drugs. That
was painful. You can be more than one person, even if they're
contradictory. But not forever.

But pain just sends you out into the night, looking for escape.

One thing that connects everyone is the drum. Europeans,
Africans, Asians, North American Indians—everyone has the
drum. As it happened, I found myself living in the midst of the
rise of electronic music and dance. I took it seriously. I was indoc-
trinated in the whole techno, house music, trance music scene. It
moved me deep in my soul.

We'd dance to this music that I had never heard but that felt
so familiar because underneath all of the bloops and bleeps and
the hi-hats and the cymbals was a drum beat. A deep bass. *Boom.*
Boom. Boom. Boom. Boom. Although I didn't recognize it at the
time, I connected with the beat in a way that triggered, deep in
my core, the same connection that Indigenous Peoples have to
the drum the world over. In a twisted colonial, inner-city way,
going to underground music warehouse parties to me felt like
how I would assume that a person dancing pow wow for the first
time might feel—it was a beautiful feeling of exhilaration,
expression, and freedom. I imagined this feeling was like the one
that hard-core pow wow dancers who put together elaborate

outfits costing thousands of dollars and travel to all the pow wows must get. It's their whole life. For me the rave scene was my whole life. It was my pow wow. The undertone. The steady beat of the drum was what made me feel so free in those moments when I would go out late at night by myself and leave behind all the other aspects of my life that were pressure. I would be in a completely free and expressive moment where I could dance, where I could express my sexuality, where I could express how beautiful I felt, where I could experience other people appreciating my beauty and movement.

The first rave I went to was in an old warehouse building, 216 Princess in Winnipeg. I had just gotten out of juvenile detention, just moved back to the city. My old friend John invited me to go to this dance party that didn't start until midnight. I asked him, "How should I dress?" And he said, "I dunno. Dress kinda pretty." And I asked him what that meant and he said to wear some nice button-up shirt and a nice pair of pants and nice shoes and do your hair really nice. So I took the last bus to downtown Winnipeg from Henderson Highway where I was living with my mother. I went to this party and it was wild. I remember dancing and hearing this music I had never heard before. It was really really good. Live DJs.

The parties would be held in old warehouses with spring-loaded floors in an old downtown neighbourhood called the Exchange District. Thick brick and mortar buildings, very old school. Back in the '90s you could rent a space in these buildings for hella cheap—a few hundred bucks would get you a few thousand square feet. They would have those big elevators with the door that would slide up and a lever you'd pull to go up and down. People of all ages from different neighbourhoods would get together and dance: bikers and Indian street gangsters, little rich kids from Tuxedo and suburban kids from Transcona, urban kids from Corydon. There were so many beautiful people there.

I got pretty wrecked at that first rave. John and I ended up doing a bunch of cocaine. I remember dancing all night until the sun came up. Of course I didn't see the sun come up because there were no windows in that warehouse space. When we left, at about five thirty in the morning, once the buses were about to start up again, the sun was bright in the sky already. In kind of a dazed trance, I walked to the museum on Main Street a couple of blocks away to catch the bus to my mother's house. I was like: *I want to do that again.* And ever since that moment, that culture, that way of expressing myself, has always been a part of my life. I have always loved dance, and I appreciate the experience of moving my body to really good music. I find it healing and I find it freeing.

Over the harsh winter that I was homeless in Winnipeg, after my mom kicked me out of her house, I'd often end up at these all-night electronic music parties because I didn't have anywhere else to go. I continued to go to a lot of parties when I was working for my brother and my uncles in the Manitoba Warriors. At the end of my shifts, I would get paid out and grab whatever I needed for the night and take off to a warehouse party. I was a tough kid but I wasn't tough like my brothers; I was never really a gangster guy. I was kind of my own thing—a skinny goth-looking teenager who wore eyeliner and powder to make my face look pale. I looked like something out of a Cure video. At a rave, a gay club, or a techno club, all of a sudden I could relax because I didn't have to be tough. It was a sanctuary where I could go and be myself. I could express myself through physical movement, fashion, hairstyle. I made a lot of friends in these scenes, and another identity started to emerge for me: a dance boy. A person who would go to raves and dance all night long.

Electronic music provided an escape from all these really damaged men who surrounded me. When a group of Native men who have been institutionalized—gone through residential school and jail, and the younger ones through juvie and jail—are living and working together in the streets of Winnipeg, quite often they become violent, even to each other. They often have a big disconnection from empathy or compassion because in all those institutions, when you show empathy, sympathy, or compassion, that's when you get hurt.

In the electronic music scene I wasn't a loser from Terrace, a screw-up who'd spent time in juvie. I could be someone and I could be beautiful. Even if you've got a little bit of a paunch like I do, you feel sexy and sexually liberated when you dance to house music, especially if you're high on ecstasy.

But it wasn't the ecstasy the changed me. The drum was pulling me back.

And there is a lesson there, which I often reflect on. Just as the rave scene drew me back to the drum, my life of anger and violence led me to healing in ways I didn't understand at the time.

I am not afraid of guys in suits, in part because I've locked eyes with hard-core criminals who could easily have thrown me out a window. I'm not intimidated by seemingly insurmountable hurdles, because I've already climbed out of a huge hole. And I don't need an MBA to get things done—I already have a PhD in hustle from the streets of the City of Dirty Water. I just needed to learn to sift the good from the bad.

And that takes me back to Terrace, and my first brushes with the law. I was given hundreds of hours of community service duty. Part of that work was to keep fire for an old Blackfoot man. I would go every Tuesday and Thursday and run his fire for his sweat lodge. He had a deal with probation so those hours could go towards my community service. At the time I thought I was doing something for him. But I know now that he was doing something for me. He was keeping a fire alive inside me.

Sex work and strip clubs and that scene was never exotic to me, because I saw the flip side. I experienced all the charms that go with that industry, that attract clientele, through the Manitoba

Warriors. It was very violent and it was not sexy. These women work hard and take great risks. I have strong opinions about the exploitation of Indigenous women in particular as a result of what I saw when I was growing up.

Because I was John's little brother, many women involved in the sex trade who were around the Manitoba Warriors saw me as the little cutie-pie. I got advice about how to treat a woman, how to make love to a woman. The sisters I hung out with while I was in the Manitoba Warriors would tell me, "Good dancers are good lovers." Often when I would finish my shift running the drug house, some of these women would say, "Hey sugar, what are your plans for the rest of the night?" And I would often jump into a cab with them and do copious amounts of cocaine and go dance all night at an after-hours club.

This made me feel like a king because I would be surrounded by all these beautiful and powerful women and they made me a better dancer, more responsive. They made me feel beautiful. I was also aware of the feeling of the eyes of those who were watching us. The more I went out to those places, the more I felt those eyes on me, and that fuelled my ego. I liked being seen. I grew up watching *Saturday Night Fever* and *Fame* and all these shows in the '80s. And I wanted to be a dancer. In some ways, that experience of feeling that people were watching me dance was a bigger high than any of the drugs I was consuming.

These friends introduced me to gay bars, like Club 200 and Happenings. Sex workers go to gay bars because after you've been doing sex work all day long, with men ogling you and paying you for services, you just want to go dance and blow off some steam. The best place to do that is at the after-hours gay bars.

Two-spirit folks, queer folks, trans folks, gay men, lesbians, members of Winnipeg subcultures, we were all hiding from something in these late-night electronic music scenes. With all of my exploration with drugs and loose morals at the time—no mentors, no guidance—the scene seemed like such a natural place to go. I didn't realize how important and liberating these places would be for me—they were safe havens for me too. A lot of straight people go to gay bars because they are sanctuaries. Nobody's going to fist-fight you in a gay bar.

At that time, I had a lot of confusion about relationships. Growing up, I didn't have a lot of healthy relationships as models. I had girlfriends when I was a kid, and my mom and all my aunties talked to me about how to treat women, but the men in my life never modelled respectful or decent behaviour. There were no long-term marriages in my family. My cousins who were siblings all had different dads. So there was a lot that I was trying to learn on the go.

I was pretty sure I wasn't gay. Many young men go through a phase where they are figuring out where they land on the spectrum of sexual preference.

In my closet, I had seven pairs of black bootcut dress pants and seven black T-shirts and a pair of ten-hole Ranger steel toe boots, shined to perfection. I had a bromance with a guy named Kyle, who was a notorious guy, very handsome. Kyle always had good fashion sense and I always wanted to look good. I told Kyle, "Give me some of your clothes and I'll give you drugs." He said, "OK, that's so cool." So I'd give him ecstasy or whatever, and I'd get a cool raver shirt. I was trying to expand my horizons, put some colour into my life.

One night I was hanging out with Kyle and his girlfriend and a woman I was dating. I said, "Yo, I got this really great liquid acid. Let's all take acid, go trip out." When we were tripping out, I got it into my head that we were tripping too hard. So I said, "I'll go to the club and sell a bunch of acid and then I'll get us a bunch of ecstasy that will level us out." My girlfriend couldn't go into the club because she was sixteen, so I said, "You guys all go trip at my apartment. I'll go to the club for an hour or two and I'll come back and see you." My girlfriend said, "All right, make sure and come meet me." Nobody had cell phones at the time.

I went to Happenings. You'd go through a door in a brick wall, up the stairs, and there was a big neon sign at the top. The place was filled with vinyl couches and booths where everybody was chilling and having drinks. On the other side of a big glass wall there was a second bar, the DJ booth, and a dance floor. It was a gay bar, so there were lots of crossdressers and gay people, mostly men, having a good time. I remember walking into Happenings, hearing house music playing, and feeling really good. I had developed an affinity for deep house music, which is big anthem music for a lot of gay bars. You could get high on ecstasy and dance to that shit all night. It's just happy—lots of deep bass notes, piano, horns.

I would always have different drugs I could trade for whatever high I wanted that night. I managed to get myself a bunch of ecstasy and then started partying. I ran into my hairstylist, a beautiful sister who worked at a fancy salon. She wore very dominatrix fashion—black patent leather and freaky colours in her hair. She smoked long More cigarettes and drove a two-seater French car. At the time, I had a Caesar cut: short and feathered forward with wisps. It was platinum, the colour of a pearl. It looked very Japanese-animation. I'd top off my dress pants and tight black Calvin Klein T-shirt with a purse that was filled with cash, mace, a straight razor, and whatever treats I was hustling.

That night, everybody was high on ecstasy and having drinks. Everybody was flirting. My hairdresser was kicking it with two other sisters who were good friends of mine. These sisters were three of the most incredibly beautiful women in the city. We were dancing in flirtatious ways on the dance floor and DJ Harry Chan, one of Winnipeg's most legendary DJs, was spinning. The whole club was just going off. I could really dance in those days, not the two-step I do now that I'm a big boy.

Derrol was on the dance floor. He's known in Winnipeg as DJ UFO. Derrol is Cree like me, and he's two-spirit. He's a beautiful Native man, very funky, a very stylish DJ. While I was dancing with my attractive female friends, I was watching this other brother on the dance floor. Not sexually, but in a very infatuated way. I was having a dance-off with Derrol. He was doing his thing and I was doing my thing. I was only thinking about his moves and then riffing on those moves, having this really beautiful exchange of energy.

In my mind Derrol was the only one in the city who could dance as good as me, who had the beat that I had. As a Native person, you connect to that bass, you connect to that drum. I believe that we fell into that world because we should have been at the pow wow dancing, but we didn't have that in our life so we found the beat in electronic music. All this real intense sexual tension was exchanging between Derrol and me and the sister friends, when I paused for a moment and looked over my shoulder and there was my girlfriend. To this day, I have no idea how she got in because you have to be over 18. She was still high on acid, a totally different vibe than the ecstasy I was on. Of course it looked real bad because—even though I was looking only at Derrol—three gorgeous women were dancing around me. My girlfriend came up to me and said, "You are coming home now."

Derrol became a very good friend. He let me know right off the bat that he had feelings for me. He would always flirt with me and over time I got to be open to it. So for a time, although Derrol and I never made it anything formal, we had a profound relationship that was more than a friendship, with elements of compassion and love and respect that felt feminine to me. When I would kick it with Derrol at the end of a big party, I didn't feel like I was cuddling with a bro. We'd be sitting in some dingy warehouse listening to whatever the last DJ was spinning at six in the morning, smoking cigarettes. Every now and then I would let him make out with me, kiss me, put his arm around me. Not because it aroused me sexually but because I loved him.

That relationship carried over a couple of years and then eventually I had to tell him, "I'm not gay. You need to move on and find someone who loves you and who appreciates you and can be what you want them to be—like you deserve them to be. But I'll always be your friend." And I have been.

A year or so later, I ran into Derrol with another friend of ours, Travis. They were on the riverbank with their arms around each other. Travis was a former best friend of mine. We had both been part of a crew of friends that had all slept with each other and shared lovers with each other. But things got complicated as they do in those kinds of circumstances. Travis and I had had a big falling-out and he started to talk shit about me. When I confronted him, he was two-faced about it. He'd be all nice to my face but then talk shit behind my back. Because we'd had a couple of bisexual encounters during group sex, when I saw him on the riverbank hanging out with the only man in my life that I ever felt the same ways emotionally about that I have felt about a woman, it was like Travis was kicking me twice in the face. Not only was he trying to attack my masculinity and how people perceived me as far as being a tough guy by saying he was going to kick my ass, but also I felt he was trying to hurt me by going for my most vulnerable, deepest darkest secret: the crush I had on Derrol.

When I saw Derrol and Travis cuddling by the river, my blood boiled. I shouted, "You!" and Travis saw me and he booked it because he knew I was going to stomp his ass. I could run like the wind back then. I caught him and I threw him to the ground and then Derrol said, "Hey man, don't be like that. I don't like seeing you this way."

I was confused. I had told this person I had feelings for that I couldn't give him what he wanted, but then seeing him trying to get what he wanted from somebody else filled me with a jealous rage. I left without beating Travis's ass that night. I felt a sense of loss and sadness that I couldn't be the guy who could treat Derrol right, who could give him all the love, all the attention and affection that he deserved. The soul that I had seen in this man and the dreams and visions and aspirations that he had shared with me showed me that he deserved nothing but love and light.

Years later, I was having a beer with Derrol. We were talking about the old days and the rave scene. He told me that my love for him when we were young men was unrequited, and that I was the one who had been pursuing him. That was a very humbling conversation that challenged my ego. I had assumed that he was madly in love with me.

So many of our Native people leave the reserve because corporations destroyed our land and they can't hunt, fish, or trap anymore. But a lot of our gay, lesbian, transgender, queer, and two-spirit relatives flee our reserves because of persecution. Our own Native people don't understand how sacred they are, the sacred role they play in the governance of our collective affairs. They bring a different perspective into our community, and they have a unique connection to the sacred. They end up in the inner city expecting to find liberation. They find it at the gay clubs, but the gay clubs are only open certain hours of the night. The rest of the time they have to deal with people who have just as much baggage as the homophobic or transphobic people on the reserve. I was lucky that I was able to go through my own experience figuring out my sexual identity. I have many relatives and know of many gay Native men who took their own life or they had their life taken from them through hate crimes. I can't say that I understand what my two-spirit brothers and sisters go through, but I empathize a little because of my romance I experienced with a man.

All people deserve to be loved and to love. And how they want to do that is none of anyone's damn business.

When Koren and I were younger, we would pack a little picnic or get a couple of coffees and a couple slices of pizza from

Henderson Café, and go to the Henderson Highway graveyard. We would fantasize about what our gravestones would look like. We've been having a lifelong argument since then. I always tell her, "Just cremate me and dump me in a river or lake or something." She always says, "Fuck that. You're going to get buried beside me." My wife is Christian, and although she doesn't practise it, she believes in Jesus Christ and she is adamant that I'm not getting cremated.

When we'd picture our gravestones, we'd imagine a spot for our family. In fantasizing about a gravestone with my wife, a shared grave, and then actually finally marrying Koren and her taking on the name Thomas-Müller, I realized that it was the beginning of an entirely new family name in this patriarchal society we live in. Part of my trying to overcome trauma in my own life and decolonize has been to take my mother's maiden name, Thomas, and to breathe new life into it. If I get it my way, there will be no sexual abuse, no physical abuse, no spiritual abuse to carry on from my generation to the next.

When I was seven, I asked Papa Harry if he'd be my dad. He said, "Yeah, sure. I'll be your dad." I asked him if he would adopt me to make it official. My mom's former partner Roddy had the opportunity to continue being my dad during the adoption proceedings, but he told the court: "If I can't have my wife, and another man is raising my son, I can't tolerate that and I don't want nothing to do with them." He signed away full custody to my mom and I never saw him again until I was an adult, when I confronted him over all the horrific things that I remember him by.

When my dear Papa Harry adopted me, I took the name Müller, but I also kept my mom's maiden name because I wanted to honour my family, where I came from. Only I, my wife Koren, and our two sons are Thomas-Müllers. For me, the name symbolizes the creation of a new family, and the ending of generations of violence on the Thomas side and the Müller side.

I see now how much is connected in that name. I am an Indigenous man. I consider it a privilege to be able to say so. That is an inheritance I take on as a responsibility to nurture. But at the same time I identify as culturally German. I love Christmas. I love to let my family sleep in so that I can go to the bakery and the deli and come back to prepare a crazy German breakfast of boiled eggs and cured meats, pickles, and a ton of different cheeses. Of course I think of myself as German. My dad was German. How could it be otherwise? One of my fondest memories is a fishing trip I took with Harry. I caught a record-breaking salmon. Harry had tears in his eyes, he was so proud. That is love. Love made me German. There is a yellowing photo of us on the wall of a tackle shop, a record of that bond.

One of the great milestones in my life was becoming a dad. Becoming a father has been very sacred. Yet the whole process of raising my two beautiful sons, Jaxson Grey and Felix Peter, at every step, every age, every major milestone that they've achieved, has been traumatizing for me because I see myself reflected in their faces. My memories attached to their particular age motivate me to do a better job than what my parents were able to do for me, given everything that they went through being Native pre-1970.

As a campaigner, you pick up a lot of emotional and spiritual luggage when you are working in affected communities, especially Native communities. Whether it's on the North Slope of Alaska, or in unceded Algonquin territory, or where I come from in northern Manitoba, or deep in the Amazon, our people are dealing with a lot of trauma. Quite often my boss at the Indigenous Environmental Network, Tom Goldtooth, would do sweat lodge ceremonies for me when I would be in his hometown, Bemidji, Minnesota, just south of Manitoba. At one of those sweat lodges, years ago, before my sons were born, I asked Tom to bring in some extra help to doctor me and help me overcome some of the weight, the pressure, the stress that I was carrying. He invited an old Anishinaabe lady to come be a part of the sweat. She came in and she prayed for me—that I could have healing and I could continue on doing the work to protect the sacredness of Mother Earth, to protect our communities.

At the end of that ceremony in the fourth round, she reached out to me in the dark and she put a wood carving in my hand and she said, "My boy, here, take this." It was a little black bear. She said, "I see two baby black bears here in the sweat lodge and they're coming to you and they're going to help you in your life in ways that you cannot possibly hope to even conceive." I didn't know what she was talking about. I thanked her, it was a good sweat, and I left. I held on to that little black bear.

I went back home to Ottawa, where Koren and I were living at the time, and two things happened not long after: Koren and I found out that we were pregnant, and my dad died. The date that the doctors gave us for our due date was the day my dad died. When the time came, Koren was in labour for hours and hours and hours. Felix was a big baby, 9.4 pounds. My wife's pelvis was separated giving birth to Felix because his head was so big. He came out and he looked like he had been boxing because he had bruises on his head where he had squeezed out into this world. During the birth, Felix inhaled some amniotic fluid and he didn't breathe for a minute. He was all blue and they were rubbing him and smacking his butt. It was the longest sixty seconds of my life. And then finally, while he was being held upside down, he screamed, and a tremendous relief washed over me.

I spent much of my life with a deep regret that my mother did not breastfeed me as a baby. White Western minds in the '70s were pushing baby formula, and so my mom fed me formula. I was wickedly allergic to it. I had all kinds of skin afflictions, cracked skin. I have terrible allergies to this day, I believe because I didn't get the antibodies that kids are supposed to get from breast milk. I have autoimmune deficiency—psoriasis, scaly skin. Many of these autoimmune issues come from disconnection from traditional food and practices, and from too much stress, both in the moment and intergenerational. Autoimmune diseases such as diabetes, psoriasis, eczema, and thyroid disorder are common among Indians, especially with all the trauma we've been dealing with. One of my biggest goals in life was to have my children breastfed. So when my first son Felix first latched on to Koren's breast and took his first meal, I could have been shot right there, dead on the spot, and I would have gone to see Creator with my head high.

When the afterbirth came out, that kid's umbilical cord was as thick as my wrist. The doctors gave me the scissors to cut his umbilical cord and it took me six or seven chops to get through it. I took his placenta and I put it in a container and the doctors all thought I was strange and they wanted to throw it away and I said, "Forget it. I've got responsibilities with that."

Planting the placenta is one of our traditions, and it is something I was never afforded when I was born. First they told my mother to abort me and she refused because she's Catholic. Then they told her to give me up for adoption and again she refused. Then the doctors told my mom not to breastfeed me, to feed me formula instead, and she did. And they threw away my afterbirth or whatever they do with it at the hospital—which is terrible because in our Indian way, the father is supposed to take that afterbirth and do a ceremony with it. It's a critical piece in the beginning of your life: to be connected to the Earth. It's as important as breastfeeding, which helps ensure that you don't have allergies, that you can fight disease, that your immune system is strong. Breastfeeding is the physical manifestation of connection to the sacred. Just as all the nutrients and antibodies a baby needs are provided in the breast milk, so the father's role is to give the baby the spiritual antibodies she or he needs, a spiritual connection to Mother Earth, through the ceremony of planting the child's umbilical cord and placenta with a pipe ceremony and cloth and spirit food offerings.

After Felix was born, I went into the nursery where my wife was sleeping and they had Felix propped up on an angle in his baby bed because his lungs were still all messed up. He was all bundled up. He had a little tuque on. He had these dark eyes and he was kind of frowning and he was looking at me. He was going "Mmmm. Mmmm. Mmmm" like a little puppy. I looked at his mom, who was passed out, exhausted. I looked back at him and he had this look in his eyes like: *I don't know who you are but I'm pretty scared right now. So do you mind holding me?* I said, "Do you want to come in here?" He came into my arms and he fell asleep.

Jaxson arrived two years after Felix. Jaxson was the result of a wild date the night after Koren decided to stop breastfeeding Felix. A week later we found out we were pregnant. A couple of days before Jaxson was born, I had a dream. In the dream, Koren was on the birthing bed in the hospital and she had her legs in the stirrups and all of a sudden a little fist went *pow!* right out of her. We got to the hospital and I was being the confident father. We had a whole birthing plan and I was telling the doctor and the nurses, "Here is our birthing plan, and don't communicate to my wife this way. The last time we were here the nurses were real mean. We want it this way." I was really adamant and I was right in the middle of explaining the plan when I got this tug on my arm and I looked back and it was one of the nurses and she said, "Excuse me, Mr. Thomas-Müller, but I'm really sorry. Your plan is out the window. She's crowning right now." I looked and I could see Jack's head coming out. I grabbed Koren's arm and she bit me on the forearm and didn't stop biting until Jack was out. I thought she was going to bite a chunk clean out, like a zombie. Luckily my walrus skin held through. We'd arrived at the hospital at 9:15 a.m. and thirty minutes later we were in the nursery with our baby.

Felix was born with his fists clenched. He was like a little tight ball. When Jack came out, they put him on my wife's chest and he stretched out. It was like he was saying: *Ahh. Thank god*

I'm out of there! He stretched and I touched his long little fingers and he opened his eyes and was like: *Oh hi, Dad.* A very old soul my son Jaxson Gray has, like he's been here before. His umbilical cord was about the thickness of my finger. It took one snip to cut it.

I had kept Felix's afterbirth so I could plant it in the earth. But I had procrastinated on doing the ceremony, and his placenta stayed in our freezer and it was a running joke for Koren and me. Anytime people would come over and look in the freezer, they would say, "What's *that?*" and we'd have a chuckle. Koren would say, "That's my placenta!" So when Jack came home, I put his placenta in the freezer with Felix's.

I'm so thankful to my wife for all that she sacrificed to give us our sons, carrying each of them for nine months. Once Koren brought Jaxson home, I hiked up to the Gatineau Hills with his older brother Felix strapped to my chest in one of those sash baby carriers with a shovel and my pipe bundle. I set him down beside me in the forest and I lit my pipe. I prayed that my sons would be connected to the sacredness of Mother Earth for the entirety of their lives, and I dug a hole and I buried their placentas together because they are brothers. I made a food offering and a cloth offering for my boys. I thought back to that time in Tom Goldtooth's sweat lodge with that old Ojibwe woman who had said that two little black bears would be coming to help me in my life, to help me in this journey. I gave thanks for her vision.

The Gatineau Hills was my sons' nursery. It's where my children grew up. Even through challenging moments over the last decade that I've been raising my kids, no matter what kind of mood my wife and I were in, if we were fighting or not, if life pressures were bearing down, big campaign crescendos coming or whatever, we would go to Gatineau Park two or three times a week, even in minus forty weather, and we would take our boys. It was only a fifteen-minute drive from our house in Ottawa. We would make sure that our boys were connected to the place where their placentas were planted in the earth. I have so many memories of Felix and Jaxson growing up on the trail, walking up the waterfall. There are grandfather trees in Gatineau Hills that are so big and old, and my sons say, "Oh, look at those grand-pas." I would always teach my sons to hug trees, not because we are environmentalists but because trees are beings. They are ancestors. They are old people. Some of the big trees, the big pines, blessed my sons. I want my boys to understand our role, our responsibilities as Native men. I try to teach my boys how to be kind, compassionate, to treat women with respect, and to treat the Earth with respect, the way you treat your mom.

Felix's Cree name is Keejick Muskwa Napui, which means Black Bear Man. Being the radical anti-capitalist, anti-colonial, anti-racist kind of guy that I grew up to be, I always swore I wouldn't give my kids Christian names. No John, no Peter, no Solomon. Pukatawagan is a Catholic community, and many have names from the Bible. But in our Cree culture, there is this really strong tradition of namesaking. They always say that when one goes, there's always one to replace them. So I namesaked my first son after my father. My son's name is Felix Peter Thomas-Müller. I always thought that was the last kick in the ass that my dad gave me from the grave. In order to keep in line with our Cree traditions, I had to go back on my commitment to not give my kids Bible names. You can never escape these Christian names. Maybe my grandkids will have Indian names. We'll see where it goes.

Raising biracial children in Canada is no easy task, especially when one of the parents is Indigenous. With centuries of systemic racism and genocide faced by my people, a lot of frustration and anger boiled to the surface during Canada's sesquicentennial celebration in 2017. That year was fraught with pain and with trauma. Not so much for me, because as an activist and as someone who reads a lot and listens to people a lot, I've developed a bit of a walrus skin. But I also have kids. My oldest son's birthday is on June 31, and we always tell him that the entire country celebrates his birthday the next day and he has a birthday week. As a family, we don't get into all the nationalism and all the pride of Canada Day. But we definitely watch the fireworks. It's a conflict. I think it's a conflict for every Native parent, because children want to see fireworks and the best fireworks are on Canada Day. It's the same thing with Christmas and Easter. When Indians participate in that stuff, it rips you in half. Because you are like: *Ahh. I'm perpetuating the colonial mindset.* While at the same time, your kids want to put decorations on a Christmas tree and have presents. They want to hunt for Easter eggs. They want to go trick-or-treating. I do my best to subversively counter those narratives that are perpetuated for a specific purpose—sowing loyalty of citizens to the agenda and ambitions of the settler-colonial state of Canada. I won't let my sons wave a Canadian flag. Instead I give them stickers and flags from Indigenous social movements, like Idle No More, to spread around. When other kids are wearing temporary tattoos of the maple leaf, my boys have a tattoo of Elijah Harper's fist holding the feather that brought down the Meech Lake Accord.

When my father died Koren and I were living in Ottawa and pregnant with Felix. I took a year off from organizing with the Indigenous Environmental Network and took a job with the National Aboriginal Health Organization. I was let go after only eight months, but the timing was perfect, as I could spend a year on unemployment insurance taking care of our newborn son.

Koren and I had chosen Ottawa because we couldn't bring ourselves to move back to Winnipeg, or not yet. We each had reasons for leaving Winnipeg. Koren works in the catering industry, and Ottawa seemed like a place where there was lots of work for chefs, and it was a good place for me politically. While living in Ottawa, I went through a lot of changes, including transitioning out of the Indigenous Environmental Network after twelve years. As Tom and I both became older, we began to fight with each other. You don't do this work without fighting, even sometimes with the people you love.

I had my German dad and he did his best, but I would always romanticize what it would be like to have a traditional Indian man as my father. One who would say, "OK, get your chores done, we've got a sweat after dinner." Or "Let's get packed up to go to the pow wow this weekend." Tom embodied a lot of those good qualities that I would fantasize about, the good qualities that I wanted to emulate when I became a father.

Working with IEN prepared me to become a dad. All the calculations and miscalculations, my conceptions about what it meant to be a man, I learned through the years that I campaigned for IEN. Much of my raw leadership, influence, and skill was sharpened by Tom's mentorship and by representing IEN's brand across Mother Earth. So after leaving the organization, I went through an identity crisis. My whole way of being had come through my role at IEN. I thought all of my strength was wrapped up in that identity, and in that little turtle that IEN has on its logo. Things reached a point where I felt it was my name taking all the shit from Tom's decisions. Growing up the way I did, the only thing I had was my name. I had built my whole life on the identity of an organization instead of confronting the demons in my past and building a stronger Clayton.

Tom and I didn't talk for a couple years, but in the end we both realized that the movement, this sacred and beautiful way, is more important than our disagreements. To this day I still call him uncle.

It's an honour to continue to work closely with IEN and be a big supporter. Even though it's been years since I moved on, I'm still part of that family. IEN is one piece of the broader movement that inspired the Native women who started Idle No More, that inspired the water protectors in Standing Rock and the Native people in Brazil who are fighting the dams. I know that

my teacher Tom and all the other OGs of the movement will
never stop. I'm proud that I inherited my resilience from them.

Some of my first fights were the result of sticking up for little
Native kids in juvie. I don't enjoy thinking about those confron-
tations. Imprisonment brings out the worst in people, guards and
prisoners alike. I saw ugly things. But when I think about those
days, I am struck by the path that leads from those little flares of
anger and violence and protectiveness to the battle for the fate of
the entire planet.

I should be clear: the fight for the fate of the planet is going
on all the time, and we're all involved. It's not just good guys and
bad guys. All of us play a role on both sides. My father Harry,
whom I love, made his fortune servicing the monstrous trucks of
the oil sands. In some sense, he is on the other side. But we all
consume more than we should. We all live a lifestyle that Mother
Earth can't sustain much longer. The point isn't to divide us up
into good guys and bad guys. We shouldn't divide at all. The
point is for all of us to find a way to act better.

Of course, not everyone sees things that way. I'm not saying
we shouldn't fight. I'm saying that the kind of victory we need is
not the kind that defeats others. It's the kind that liberates. That
may sound like an empty distinction, but it's not. I don't fight for
greed. I don't even fight for myself. I fight against the Winter
Spirit, the rapacious force that tears communities apart. If I win,
we will be free from that spirit of endless hunger and selfishness.

And when you don't fight for yourself, you can put your ego
aside.

For years before I joined 350.org, I didn't like that organization, and I know they didn't like me. We were openly hostile. I
thought their approach of peddling carbon credits and forest off-
sets was a fraud, and I said so. Their agents were running around
the Amazon, showing up in remote villages offering to buy their
trees (or worse, bulldozing them and planting fast-growing

monocrops like palm). I thought that was just another form of colonization, and I said so. The bottom line is that paying money for the privilege of trashing the planet—which is pretty much the definition of a carbon offset—is just another luxury for the global middle class. And trampling all over Indigenous Peoples' land and way of life just makes it worse. And I said so.

So no, I did not get along with the wealthy kids from 350.org who had slick PowerPoints and easy access to policy-makers, as well as a message that a lot of people wanted to hear: you can keep doing what you're doing, it's just going to cost you a *little* more money. Even their name seemed to get it wrong: "350" stands for the safe concentration of carbon dioxide in the atmosphere: 350 parts per million. (We're at well over 400 right now, by the way.) This approach reduces the environment to a chemistry problem. It says that there is an appropriate level of destruction to wreak on Mother Earth. I called bullshit on them. I was the IEN hatchet man.

But everything shifted in 2009. That was the year the American Clean Energy and Security Act was passed by Congress. It was better known as the Waxman-Markey bill, and it was a disaster from an environmental and sovereignty point of view. It was so watered down by the energy lobby, and so bloated with special provisions, that IEN was against it. But it did contain the basic framework of a carbon-trading scheme, which in theory would force American companies to limit emissions, which would bring the US into line with the EU and put it in a leadership position as the world tried to steer the supertanker of the global economy in a direction more consistent with the Kyoto Accord.

But of course even that weak legislation was never sent to the Senate for debate and so it never became law. That was a huge slap in the face for a coalition known as One Sky, which comprised the big environmental groups like the Sierra Club and Greenpeace.

Environmental NGOs are always trying to co-opt First Nations. Everyone wants to be able to say they work with First

Nations, but they don't want to be transparent and accountable to First Nations. IEN and their allies created a counterculture in the NGO world, with NGO groups that had learned how to work and be accountable, not just to the Native communities, but to themselves and to the country on the whole, to people across the planet. We were able to create a coalition of smaller organizations that incorporated human rights into their work, into their analyses, into their high-level political statements and objectives. Today almost every Greenpeace press release includes in the top three points: "Respect the free, prior, and informed consent of the First Nations." This is a big thing for these big environmental groups to say. Some people would say they are co-opting our strategy; I would say they are learning from the ridiculous mistakes they've made in the past and buckling under the pressure of the people power that we've established through social movement organizing.

Groups like IEN had always had an arm's-length relationship with groups like that. There is nothing in their mandates that acknowledges our sovereignty or our interests. For the most part, Indians could vanish off the face of the Earth as long as the seals are safe. So we weren't exactly allies, even though we were all environmentalists in name. We thought they were part of the problem, and I'm sure they felt the same about us.

The failure of Waxman-Markey changed all that.

While the legacy environmentalists were taking Beltway staffers out to dinner, the IEN was engaging tribal leaders to fight the Keystone XL pipeline. Nothing proves the way everything is connected like a pipeline. Of course it connects the tar sands in Alberta to the refineries of Texas. But it also connects every tribe and nation from the muskeg of northern Alberta to the Gulf Coast. We turned that connection into our strength.

We looked at a map and we traced the route of the proposed right-of-way. Then we reached out to each and every council along the pipeline's route. We got lawsuits and protests going over a range of issues, from water contamination to treaty rights to violations of prescribed consultation processes. It was the right fight to join. The route would go through the heart of the continent, across the Ogallala Aquifer. The water table is so high in some spots that the meadows are underwater for months. This is water that feeds many rivers and cities and Native communities in water-scarce areas.

The whole thing was a bad idea, and just about everyone we talked to saw that. Marty Cobenais, IEN KeyXL campaigner, did a circuit ride along the proposed pipeline route and laid the foundation for the Cowboy Indian Alliance while at the same time acquiring over a dozen tribal council resolutions—that is, tribal laws—opposing the mega-project. We had tribal leaders committed to chaining themselves to the White House fence. We had the date lined up: September 14, 2011.

It was at that point that Bill McKibben, one of the founders of 350.org, called me.

"Hey man. I heard you're going to have this day of action. I wanted to talk to you."

I was suspicious. "Glad you like our campaign . . ."

He said, "Look, maybe we can work together on this campaign. Instead of a day of action headed up by tribal leaders, why don't we collaborate on a whole week with citizens from every corner of the United States risking arrest?"

We talked for a while, and eventually we agreed. My one deal-breaker was that the last day had to be Native day, and the last person to get arrested was going to be an Indian from the right-of-way. The result was the biggest protest in Washington since Vietnam. We had more than 160,000 people in the streets.

From that point on, I started getting tighter with 350.org, and so did the IEN. I loved the sheer scale of their operation, their budget and outreach. And I loved that they listened. I could see that they understood that climate change is not just a scientific problem. They could see that it's a question of justice, and of community, and about the innate value of what we are fighting to protect, rather than just an abstract idea of "sustainability."

More and more, we were seeing eye to eye. Together, we staged another event at the White House, surrounding it with protesters holding hands, four rows deep. We brought out Daryl Hannah and Neil Young to the New York Climate March, where UN secretary-general Ban Ki-moon called for a climate summit. We were on a roll.

Tom Goldtooth and I had a bit of a falling-out. He is a hard man. He is a fighter, not a diplomat. He never wanted to be a diplomat. I respect that, but it makes him a hard guy to work with. So we respectfully parted ways. IEN would lead the Keystone fight, and I would partner with the Polaris Institute and fight the tar sands. I was also doing a lot of work with Idle No More at that time. I was still very public in the Keystone fight, but it was 350.org that would fly me down to the US.

One day I got a call from May Boeve, the executive director at 350. She said, "We're doing a vigil in New York tonight. Can you come down?" Of course I said yes. A few hours later I was at LaGuardia, hopping into a cab to head into Manhattan. There I gave a twenty-minute speech about why Obama had to stop Keystone. And then I was done. All the adrenaline of the day ebbed out of me.

May and I were in a taxi heading over to Brooklyn, where the 350 office is (and where my hotel was), when she turned the conversation towards work.

"I assume you heard—we're starting an office in Canada to fight the tar sands?"

I said yeah, I'd heard. I heard my young friend Cam Fenton was going to run it.

We rode along in silence a little. Then an idea popped into my head like a spark coming off a campfire. I said, "What do you think about me coming on board?"

Soon I was on board.

And I love it. It's a totally different experience from planning campaigns around a volunteer's kitchen table, pulling in favours, and managing relationships. (It's a small world, and the question of who has slept with whom can really complicate things.) With 350, we had the in-house firepower to go toe to toe with giants like Energy East, Kinder Morgan, and the Royal Bank of Scotland. We have 160 staff in 80 countries. We have in-house artists, coders, lawyers. And my first action with 350 showed how we could use that muscle.

At the March for Jobs, Justice and Climate on July 5, 2015, in Toronto, we brought together ten thousand people from the labour movement, social justice organizations, women's groups, groups working for justice for murdered and missing Indigenous women, and many more. On the day of the march, we had professional medics and marshals on the ground. We had media and police liaisons. We had the momentum to shift the Overton window. We weren't nearly on the multi-billion-dollar scale of the banks, energy companies, and investment funds we were looking to checkmate, but we at least had the scale to get the message out and to change the way people talk about climate justice.

Of course, it also changed the way people talk about *me*. I've started to hear that I've sold out. That I've gone to work for a "white" NGO. I shouldn't be surprised. I've seen more than my share of lateral violence and rivalry. But I know in my heart that we're all on the same team. Not just 350 and IEN and all the grass-roots organizations that spring up to fight energy projects. I mean labour and migrants and trans rights groups and everyone who shows up when the drums start at every march. Some mainstream environmentalists might ask what fighting a pipeline has to do with LGBTQ rights. But I know that everything is connected.

iskotêw

———————

ᐃᓄᑫᐤᐤ

———————

fire

was talking to my grandmother GiGi, the mother of my mother, one day, asking her what she knew about our culture and tradition. She told me that when she was a little girl, her grandfather George Nicolas showed her his bundle and his pipe. George was a medicine man and he was known for fasting underneath the ice in the winter. He had a pipe and he showed that to my grandmother and he told her, "My girl, I'm not going to give this to you or any of your brothers or sisters because your life is going to be really hard and a lot of you are going to die horrible deaths. But I promise you, my girl, that your children's children will pick up this stuff again." And he pointed at his bundle.

Talking to her made me think of Dave Courchene, an Elder here in Manitoba. His message is that the prophecy of the seventh fire—which is the Anishinaabe version of the Cree prophecy of the seventh generation—is complete. Now it's time to light the eighth fire. The generation after the prophesied seventh generation is coming of age.

Seventy-five percent of Inuit, Métis, and First Nations people are under the age of thirty. Fifty-five percent are under the age of twenty-five. There's a coming transference of economic power, consumer power, to the most marginalized populations in Canadian society. There were 450 Indigenous graduates from the University of Manitoba in 2018 alone. This population is rapidly ascending into the workforce and will account for one out of every four workers contributing to the Canadian GDP. This is the biggest transference of economic buying power to Natives, who wield immense economic influence. This population is the most sophisticated, educated, empowered, and self-determining they've been since before colonialism.

I interpret this rise of the Native as the manifestation of the eighth fire prophecy. Our Elders saw this moment, and through prophecies, they talked about a generation of our young people who would be free from the colonial mindset and would lead our people to a place of abundance and freedom.

I was the first of GiGi's grandchildren. There are hundreds of us now—grandchildren and great-grandchildren and great-great-grandchildren. When I was born, my mom named me after my great-great-grandfather George Nicolas. I'm Clayton George Thomas-Müller. I had two uncle Georges namesaked after my great-great-grandfather, and they both died horrible deaths at a young age, just like my great-grandfather said they would. But I'm the fourth-generation George and I'm still here. I was the first one in my family, after colonization, to Sundance, and I was the first one to become a pipe carrier.

The pipe is the key that unlocks ceremony. The pipe links us to the land. It connects us to the ancestors that came before us. It connects us to each other. And it grounds us as we make commitments to the generations to follow. The sweat lodge, the Sundance, and every prayer to Creator—these acts of love and forgiveness and solemn promise are sealed by the pipe.

I take very seriously this movement and this work and this life that I've been given in the City of Dirty Water. I feel that, as young people who are part of the prophecy of seven generations, we are prophecy living, we are prophecy manifested in real time. We have big work to do to repair our relationship with the sacredness of Mother Earth, with each other as humanity. We have to heal these scars on Mother Earth, and make our cities sustainable. It's our responsibility to our ancestors and our children.

The most renewable energy on the planet is not solar energy. It's the human capacity for love, kindness, and forgiveness. That's the fuel that drives me. I convert my anger into love. When I see my kids or other little children, and the people that I care about and even my people on the street, I convert that anger into loving them. That's where I get my inspiration.

I have been gifted with beautiful children. I get my daily inspiration, first and foremost, from my sons. I get up every day with them, at five thirty in the morning. I make them breakfast and we start our morning together. It doesn't matter if I was working until four in the morning, I get up with them.

My wife inspires me all the time. She's my best friend and I'm deathly afraid of her.

My family inspires me because they continue to survive through hard times. I have so many cousins and aunties and uncles and blood relatives who suffer every day: poverty, addiction, incarceration, and suicide. Love and inspiration come from these things too, though that love hurts. Love requires of us that we feel another's pain, as well as her joy or his contentment. We need the courage to be true to our love.

The sacred way of life that we have as Native people, the Sundance way of life, the path of kindness and unconditional love, inspires me.

I did not walk that path alone. There were many ahead of me leading the way, many beside me to lean on when I stumbled. There was tradition to shed light when all seemed dark. There were ancestors whose honour made burdens lighter. So while I am proud, that does not mean that the credit is mine to claim.

What it means is that even the gross injustices and cruelties I have seen are only starting in some places. They are where we can take our first steps towards where we want to be. And they're the places we'll find our brothers and sisters who need us. But they are not cut off from the bright lights of lecture halls, or comfortable suburbs, or wherever you are reading this book. They are all connected.

I have spoken as an Indigenous man, as an activist, as someone seeking the correct spiritual path through a landscape pocked and pitted by traps, many of them centuries old, some as old as the world, some of my own creation. I have sought my own way of becoming a warrior. But mine are not the only ways.

As Indigenous Peoples, as workers, as environmentalists, as people who want to do the right thing, we cannot fight and win these battles on our own. We need allies. It is time to come out of our silos, to link arms, and to forge a common front against the tyranny of corporate power, against the shadow of the Winter Spirit. That's what became clear to me in New York. Was it revenge I wanted, or justice? They're not the same thing. I had been on a path from the criminal detention system to the world of crime, to 350.org, where I could cross paths with others who wanted justice as passionately as I did. People who could help me. People who could help, period. It would be selfish to feed my anger when there was so much to do and so many opportunities to do it.

These are times when revolutions are many, but our energies must be harnessed and directed appropriately. We must bring together the right combination of vision, strategy, and democratic organizing with a convergence of different movements putting forward a clear vision for radical transformation. As my friend Naomi Klein often says, it's going to take all of us to change everything.

Winnipeg has a bad reputation—Stab City, Stab Peg, Racist Peg. A couple of years ago, *Maclean's* magazine put Winnipeg on its cover as the most racist city in Canada. We need to change that. I have big hopes for the City of Dirty Water. All across the world, I've seen what's possible when communities come together. You see it in Detroit. You see it in Pittsburgh. You see it in Cleveland. All these Rust Belt cities that collapsed in the wake of global trade deals. Winnipeg is similar. It lost a lot of its population, but now it's the fastest-growing city in Canada. When I left Winnipeg in 2004, there were fewer than 700,000 people; as I write this, there are almost 850,000.

Because of the rail economy that's coming back as a result of climate change, there's going to be massive investment in fossil-free transportation of goods and services. Governments and industry have big ambitions for the central corridor of continental North America. Winnipeg used to be the big city of trains, and I believe they'll come back again. I believe Winnipeg will be a central hub for food production, for the manufacturing of textiles and hardware for the emerging zero-carbon energy economy. I have dreams about how Indigenous people will contribute to the economy of Winnipeg by building the factories of tomorrow, creating tens of thousands of jobs not just for Native people but for all people living in Winnipeg. We'll do it in our urban reserves, like the former Kapyong Barracks that the Treaty 1 chiefs acquired in 2019 through the Treaty Land Entitlement process. These are urban tax-free business development zones where we will control the economics under our own sovereignty and self-determination. Not only can we use the renewable resources from our lands to become the backbone of economic recovery from climate change for our peoples, we can also drive this change through massive job creation in other lands we acquire through Treaty Land Entitlement and the production we create in these places of things like micro-hydro, wind turbines, solar panels, battery technology, and, who knows, maybe electric vehicles and trains.

We'll partner with Manitoba and with the civic government of Winnipeg and make deals to create economic self-determination. Through economic self-determination, we can achieve self-determination of community, sovereignty, and true nationhood. We should not have to sacrifice the quality of the air, the climate, the water to put food on the table, to put opportunity in the hands of people who want opportunity. We should be able to pursue economic development in a way that solidifies our place in the sacred circle of life. Our economic opportunities should be born from a place of restoration of the biosphere, of regeneration.

Our extraction should follow simple rules, what my old mentor Tom Goldtooth called the original instructions—for instance, if we take something, we must put something back.

I want to build an economic paradigm in Manito Ahbee— the sacred place where Creator sat—that is bio-regionally planned, that asserts our territorial jurisdiction as Indigenous Peoples. I want to work with First Nations in the urban reserve in Winnipeg to create jobs not just for Native people but for all Manitobans working in Native-owned manufacturing centres that are producing renewable energy infrastructure to transition Canada away from fossil fuels. I want to support our Native people to get involved in green chemistry, to explore the applications of textiles made from hemp and other products that make sense for the massive infrastructure transition required to address climate change.

I want to support our First Nations communities to adjust their revenue streams with the federal government. It wouldn't take a lot to figure out the supply chain of the Canada Mortgage and Housing Corporation, which owns all of the First Nations homes in our reserves and is responsible for maintaining existing stock and building new stock, and to make some minor adjustments so that we are building climate-sane homes, homes that make sense within the context of our biosphere. It wouldn't take much adjusting to build homes that use the sun for passive heating. It wouldn't take much to build homes that have geothermal radiant heat throughout. The federal government has a fiduciary and legal obligation to us. It makes $8 billion in transfer payments every year. How do we take a look at all of those revenue streams coming into Manitoba and adjust them slightly so that we can eliminate energy bills and build houses that last for a hundred years?

A true revolutionary is somebody who discovers a negative revolution in the cycle of time and puts an end to it and replaces it with a positive. Everything that has happened will happen again. Nothing ever really changes, unless a very brave individual, or a strong family, organizes a social movement to change it.

I've started growing a garden in my backyard and it's beautiful. At dinnertime, I tell Felix, "Go and get some kale from the garden." He runs out with a basket and he cuts some kale. There's great power in being able to harvest our own food. I want all our Native people to have that, to grow gardens and address the food poverty in their communities. It's hard to be creative when you're stressed out about feeding your kids. It's hard to be creative when you're stressed out about fines and interventions of the state into your life. It's hard to be creative when you're trying to overcome colonial trauma. And it's really hard to heal from all the trauma if you're constantly spinning your wheels to put food on the table, to pay the bills.

A garden is a connection to the Earth. We care for the Earth, and she cares for us. Where we are matters; the land that we stand on matters. It matters, but it is not ownership in the European sense. It was here before us and it will be here when we're gone. We do not own it. It makes more sense to say that it owns us. But we can live each day knowing that our relationship is one of tenderness and respect.

For me it is also an act of forgiveness. It is the warrior's way. It is turning anger into love. It is a sort of reconciliation, and an end to lateral violence.

All this is a lesson I learned from my first stepdad. Roddy was half Carib and he always identified with the Black side of his family, but I'm certain that his mother was Mohawk. As soon as springtime hit one year, Roddy went out to the backyard of our house on Evergreen Boulevard. He tilled the entire yard and turned the soil over. He planted corn. As an adult, remembering this, I always thought that was his Mohawk side coming out. Mohawks, like many of our nations, share a connection with corn. Come the fall, our entire backyard was filled with two-metre-high stalks of corn. Roddy was gone by the time the corn was ready to harvest, but I remember eating the corn all winter, and thinking fondly of him. He was a dangerous, violent, terrifying man who allowed his demons to grievously harm those he loved. But in his garden, I saw him create instead of destroy.

I know for a fact that his ability to become more than his demons was rooted in his Native identity. Roddy also loved calligraphy. The one thing I kept from our years together was a scroll he had penned and glued to a piece of moosehide. He had copied a quote from Chief Dan George. I've lost it in the years that have passed since then, but I remember the message well: To help others, you have to fix yourself. I think it works the other way too. If you want to fix yourself, helping others will teach you the way. There is no healing by yourself.

When I moved out on my own at the tender age of fourteen, things got really difficult, but there was beauty in the journey and I made a lot of good friends. I ended up living with my first girlfriend and her family for one winter on the Kitsumkalum reserve, just outside Terrace, BC. It was a beautiful experience. Her dad told me that he was a California Indian and I thought he was just incredible. He fought in Vietnam and he had fallen in love with her mom, a beautiful Tsimshian woman.

Her dad would come barrelling into the boys' room in the middle of the night, yelling: "Get up! I got a moose! I need you boys to gut this thing. I want it cut up by the sunrise!" We'd all trek outside and there would be a moose strung up and we'd have to take it apart. I will always owe a debt to that man, even though he was a little bit loopy from his Vietnam experience. Through him, I got some pretty good lessons on how to be a bushman. I learned to have a deeper connection to that land in the Skeena Valley. He had his trauma, and I had mine, but together we learned.

Many of my teenage years were spent in pristine wilderness, in places where you could drink right from the stream. You could pick fiddleheads and eat them raw. There was an abundance of food, all kinds of berries: huckleberries, raspberries, salmonberries, blackberries. There was incredible biodiversity and wildlife. On the coast you could dig razor clams and pick oysters and mussels from the rocks. That land instilled in me a deep respect for ecology and almost a fundamentalist need to defend it so that future generations could benefit from it.

Years later when I became a climate justice organizer, one of the main campaigns I worked on was fighting against Enbridge, a pipeline company that tried to build a massive pipeline from the Alberta tar sands to the Pacific Northwest port of Kitimat—which would have cut a swath right across the area where I grew up. They wanted to drill through mountains for this pipeline, all to get tar sands oil to international markets. If they had succeeded, their pipeline would have crossed more than twelve hundred salmon-producing rivers and streams. A leak could have poisoned all those rivers and streams. We defeated them.

Today I get out on the land as often as I can. I'm so grateful for the privilege I have to go for our annual brothers' hunt in the homeland of my sister Leona Starr-Manoakeesick. Thunderchild First Nation is so beautiful, way up in northern Saskatchewan, Treaty 6 territory. I often dream about the land there, the coulees, the beautiful ridges where you can see for miles and miles. All the poplar and spruce trees and birch trees. It's an incredible place that provides me with the opportunity to give meat to my grandmother GiGi and to feed my sons, Jaxson and Felix, wild meat from the land. The river at Thunderchild and the valley that we hunt in for elk and moose is the river that flows up to my own community, Pukatawagan. We are connected by water.

Being out at a hunt and having a successful hunt and taking apart the animal, hanging the moose's bell—the long beard that hangs under its jaw—facing north to honour its spirit, its pride, are all experiences that you have to do when you grow up in the city.

You've got to really work hard to go out onto the land. If you don't have connection to the First Nation where you are registered or where your parents are registered, you need to make friends, build a circle of community, so you can get out onto the land, get your hands bloody taking apart an animal, go out harvesting medicines—the sacred sages, the rat root. The sacred places exist, but it takes hard work and months and months of planning to get to them. But it's well worth it, because these are the experiences that give you the energy you need to overcome the hard times that you might face growing up in a city across these lands they call Canada.

I believe in prophecy. There's a Cree story about an old man who had a vision about giants who were marching from the north to the south, and in their hands they carried the power of the Thunder Beings. He said that when that march of the giants from the north to the south happened, the people of the land would get very sick. What he saw were the massive transmission lines, the power lines that carry the hydroelectric energy from the dams in northern Quebec to the south—they look like giants.

I find myself at a crossroads as I reflect on my life. I'm tired and I want to get inspiration from more hopeful themes, to build something instead of just battling. It's a good fight and I've done my part and I'll continue to do my part as long as I'm asked to, without question. But I would like to dream into a vision for a new economic paradigm in Manitoba.

I've always had Manitoba Hydro squarely in my crosshairs to hold them to account for what they did to our sacred lands and waters. I never understood how deeply I was affected by mega-dams flooding my family's homelands until my adult life. I ended up in Winnipeg because of it. I would like to spend the next part of my life decommissioning all those dams. I would like to make the energy they produce unnecessary by supporting our First Nations communities to install solar and wind power. In our communities, 38 percent of household income goes to heating homes, because the houses are so shitty. I want to work with our First Nations peoples to introduce less invasive forms of technology and address our energy poverty.

As we look at global problems, like the end of the era of cheap energy and the loss of natural capital to sustain this ridiculous economic paradigm called capitalism, and of course catastrophic climate change, we have to globalize justice in the interest of localizing power. We have to get rid of this centralization of power that's happened in our energy systems, in our food production and distribution, in all the systems that we are dependent upon. This transformation is possible.

This is the focus of the work of the environmental justice and Indigenous rights social movements. Not just stopping the bad guys from expanding the tar sands or building the pipelines that will lock our economy into a dirty-fossil-fuel-dependent economic paradigm for another century, but starting to support communities to explore other ways of creating sustainability. Since the beginning of colonization Indigenous Peoples have been trying to communicate to the colonizer that everything is inextricably connected. In 250 years of industrialization, colonizers have almost destroyed our ability to live on Mother Earth. Integrated, holistic governance of our nations, our cities, and the relationship that they have with the land and resources is how we are going to do it. We can achieve this through developing local food security programs, community cold storage, and local food distribution—economic opportunities led by cooperatives of communities and tribal nations across the medicine line between Canada and the US. We can do all those things and lead a renewable energy revolution and end the colonial relationship our nations have been trapped in. That is one way sovereignty issues and environmental campaigns are related. An unsustainable infrastructure has grown up around our nations, in Manitoba no less than in Oklahoma, and it has fallen to us to fuel these monsters. Government and capitalists should not be coming to us for handouts.

When I was a small child, my mother took me to an Elder so that I could receive my spirit name. My ancestors will recognize me only by that name. I forgot it. But it was not lost. It was given back to me at my first Sundance. The things that pass through our hands can come back to us, if they are important enough.

When I learned my spirit name, I learned my clan and the colours that go with it. Now, when I pray at Sundance, I bring a yard each of blue, black, purple, and red broadcloth and bind them to a tree. With this, I announce my intention and take my place.

As I've said before, the teaching that the Eagle clan must carry to the world is love. The eagle flies the highest and sees the farthest. I have much more to see, and much more to learn. But what I can see, from the modest height I have attained, is that scared little kid I once was, that bewildered little Cree kid who didn't know whether he belonged in Puk or in Winnipeg, who couldn't always differentiate between those who would protect him and those who would hurt him, who couldn't see the difference between anger and justice. From a certain height, you see time laid out like space, like a landscape. And there is young, confused Clayton.

From that height, one also sees others, and the confusion and violence that shaped them. Isn't that love? Isn't that forgiveness? Knowing that the others' anger and rapacity is not so different from one's own? That it reaches out from the past to blight the present—if we let it? That the love-killing Winter Spirit dwells in all of us—if we let it? That it is not for us to condemn our brothers and sisters but to stare down that cold, bitter spirit?

That is the warrior's love.

But why would the eagle look only to the past? There is much to admire in the past, and much to celebrate. And there is the responsibility placed on our shoulders by our ancestors. But our ancestors point us in the direction of the future. Our responsibility lies in moving forward.

From the eagle's height, the future is laid out like a map. Strength will return to us, but also wisdom. Yes, we have stumbled. But so have others. Others have much to learn, even as we remember it. The eighth generation will be teachers.

And we will be warriors. We will need to rely on our strength, and our strength may rely on our anger. But we must not allow our anger to consume us or tempt us to become the thing we are fighting. The warrior must not tread his brothers and sisters underfoot. He is a protector, not a despoiler. Warriors are not defined by fighting. They are defined by fighting *for*.

That is what life in the City of Dirty Water has taught me. So far. Now I have more to learn.

ACKNOWLEDGMENTS

I want to acknowledge my mother for giving me permission to share these stories of growing up Indigenous in these lands that they call Canada. I know it has been very hard for you, Mom, to have witnessed me go through this recollection of trauma in my healing journey.

I want to acknowledge my late father, Peter Sinclair Sr., and just say I love you, Dad, and I'll see you in the good hunting grounds when my time here on Mother Earth is complete.

My sons, Peter Felix Thomas-Müller and Jaxson Gray Thomas-Müller: this entire storytelling universe that I've named Life in the City of Dirty Water is a gift to you that you can share with my grandchildren once I become an ancestor. Stories change the world; they inspire people to greatness and they facilitate the healing of our body, spirit, and mind. The art of storytelling is a gift that I pass on to you.

I want to acknowledge my production team: my co-editor, Anna Lee-Popham, and fellow co-director and executive producer of the film *Life in the City of Dirty Water*, Spencer Mann. Without your kind and generous guidance, facing my inner demons and trying to break colonization's grip on my mind and spirit would not have been possible. You two are truly, truly best friends for life.

I also want to acknowledge Cam Fenton, who worked with me for over a decade, challenged me to become a better writer, and introduced me to the staff at Page Two Books. Page Two took this memoir to the next level and opened the door to Penguin Random House Canada. Specifically, I would like to name Amanda Lewis, for her help in facilitating the publication of *Life in the City of Dirty Water*. I want to acknowledge Nicholas Garrison, my editor at Penguin, who showed much passion for editing my story. I really appreciated our emotion-filled talk about our fathers. And I want to acknowledge and thank my agent, Carolyn Forde at Transatlantic Agency, who is exquisitely professional and a true champion in her field.

I want to acknowledge Christi Belcourt and Isaac Murdoch for providing such incredible art, including the cover of this book. Our ancestors love beauty and colorfulness, and you both continue to bring so much of that into the world.

It's been really tough growing up with so many of our Indigenous men being so broken. Having so many failed attempts of men in my life took a toll on my ability to be a father to my sons. But I want to thank all the men I've called Dad in my life, especially my adopted dad, Harry Thomas-Müller, whom to this day I continue to call Papa and is an incredible Opa to my sons.

I want to thank the community who surrounds me, all of my dearest friends: Brennan, Stuart, Parry, Mike, and all of our extended Sundance family. I would not be alive to tell this story if it were not for the Sundance way of life and my Sundance family.

Koren Lenore Thomas-Müller, you are and will forever be my greatest source of inspiration, my greatest passion, my greatest love. You are the best mother to our little bears and I'm so happy to share with you the life-long journey of raising our sons to be better than I had ever hoped to be.

Howay. It feels like I'm writing my will here. But I still got lots of life in me.

This memoir represents a new phase in my life as I enter middle age and I hope it will spark a conversation about what it will actually take to heal both Indigenous Peoples and non-Indigenous peoples in Canada and across Mother Earth. It's my hope that these conversations will help undo the great wrongs that have been inflicted by colonization, patriarchy, and white supremacy.

I have great faith in young people and the future.

Ekosan Maha,

Ki Na Na Skomitnowwow,

Clayton George Thomas-Müller
Strong Thunderbird Man